CALENDAR
Garden

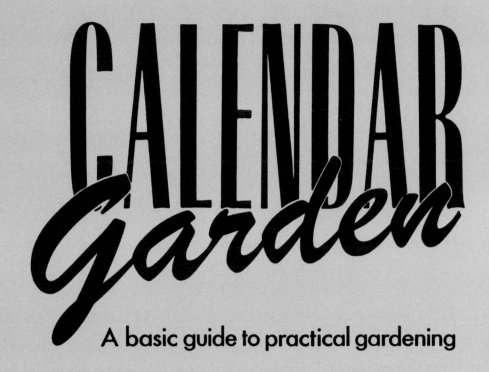

CALENDAR Garden

A basic guide to practical gardening

ALAN MASON & MARYLYN WEBB

WARD LOCK LIMITED · LONDON

ACKNOWLEDGEMENTS

The publishers are grateful to the following for granting us permission to reproduce the following photographs: Alan Mason (pp 19, 27, 46 (top and bottom), 47 (top), 51, 55, 62, 66, 71, 75, 87 and front cover (top right)); Garry Atkinson (pp 18, 22, 26, 39, 82, 83 and front cover (bottom rignt)); the Harry Smith Horticultural Photographic Collection (pp 35, 47 (bottom)); and Yorkshire Television (back cover). The left-hand front cover picture and photograph on p.23 were taken by Bob Challinor, courtesy of Arthur Billitt of Clack's Farm.

All the line drawings were drawn by Pamela Dowson.

Based on the Calendar gardening programme; Director, Gary Ward; Executive Producer, Graham Ironside.

Photographs courtesy of: Garry Atkinson, Alan Mason, Yorkshire Television Stills Department.

© Alan Mason & Marylyn Webb 1987

First published in Great Britain in 1987 by Ward Lock Limited, 8 Clifford Street London W1X 1RB, an Egmont Company

House editor Denis Ingram
Text set in Gill Sans Light by Hourds Typographica, Stafford, England

Printed and bound in Spain by Cayfosa, Barcelona
Dep. Leg. B-43195-1986

British Library Cataloguing in Publication Data

Mason, Alan
    Calendar garden.
    1. Gardening
    I. Title   II. Webb, Marylyn
    635   SB450.97

    ISBN 0-7063-6534-8

CONTENTS

INTRODUCTION

Why does the world need another gardening book? To be honest, the *world* probably does not, but this book is not intended to solve all the world's gardening problems. It sets out to show how to start a garden from scratch, either a new one, or an old one renovated, and how to overcome the special problems created by a northern climate. So, if you want to conquer the world in gardening, this is probably not the complete work you are seeking. But if you are new to gardening or new to your present garden, then what follows should be the down-to-earth guide you need.

Gardener versus Northern Climate

If you can garden well 'Up North' then you can garden well anywhere! The northern climate does not encourage adventurous gardening – but it does provide a worthwhile challenge. While we dare not attempt to grow some of the tender plants which thrive and flourish 'Down South', even in sheltered locations, this should not discourage any attempt to grow *slightly* tender specimens. All that is needed is greater determination and care.

Later springs and earlier autumns conspire to reduce the growing season: early plantings have to contend with late frost (a different beast altogether from late frost in southern climes); winters are longer, and temperatures lower. So we have to try harder to achieve good results.

Most gardening books – this being one of the rare exceptions – are based on the southern growing season. So northern gardeners should check recommended planting times for instance, warily.

The northern garden tends to be two to three weeks behind its southern cousin in spring, and autumn arrives two to three weeks early. Its two biggest enemies are wind and frost. Leaves can be scorched, and even ripped to shreds. So plants in exposed gardens crave shelter. A solid fence or wall, however, is not the answer; wind hitting a solid barrier sets up turbulence, creating eddies, which cause more problems than the unimpeded wind would have done.

While winter frosts can be deadly, often it is the spring frost, just at the time when plants are emerging from hibernation, which can cause most distress. To see a plant starting into new growth stirs a sense of eagerness and excitement in any gardener's heart – so to wake one morning to find a mass of shrivelled, frosted leaf tips is disheartening, to say the least! It is possible to give plants some winter protection by building a wigwam of bracken, straw or clipped yew branches (Fig. 1). If protected during their first two seasons, young, tender plants do become hardier and settling them in well does give them a fighting chance of survival. But this form of 'protection racket' is only feasible for individual plants. It is possible to help the rest of the garden by sensible planting.

Fig 1 Wigwam of bracken or yew branches to protect tender plants over winter.

With a sloping garden, whether steep or gentle, remember that just as hot air rises, cold air sinks, Therefore, if there is a barrier at the foot of a sloping garden it will trap cold, frosty air running down the slope and form a frost pocket. Planting which allows the frost to escape will greatly benefit the whole garden (Fig. 2).

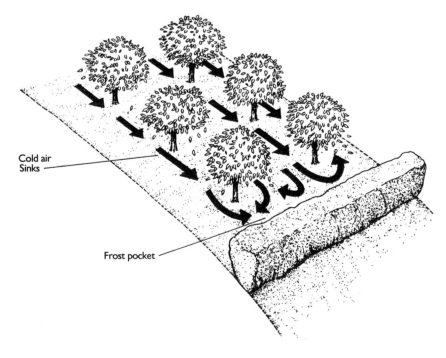

Cold air Sinks

Frost pocket

Fig. 2 On a sloping site frost travels downhill forming a frost pocket. Careful siting of trees allows unhindered flow of cold air. Removal of solid barrier (hedge) would allow frost to disperse.

7

1 PREPARATION

Don't rush into anything! Hasty decisions could cost time and money in the long run. First, make a sketch of the proposed garden – including the house and the positions of the windows. So much garden viewing is done from the house, so why not have the best views from the windows? Also, try to think of the garden as an outdoor room. A lot of care and thoughtful planning go into decorating the house, choosing colour schemes, etc., and the garden deserves the same attention.

Some gardens are much easier to plan than others. A picture comes to mind immediately of the desired effect. Others can take weeks to formulate, and, unless it is a very formal plan, it is almost impossible to design the ideal garden immediately. So sit down with the sketch and a note pad, and ask yourself the following questions:

Who is the garden for?
A garden suitable for a middle-aged couple will not necessarily be ideal for a young family. With children around it might be better to reduce the size of the herbaceous border and increase the lawn and vegetable plot.

What is its aspect?
Does the garden face north, south, east or west? This is vital when deciding what plants to incorporate. The same applies to walls, whether house or garden walls, A south-facing aspect gives more scope for a wider variety of plants.

Is it to be an inward or outward facing garden?
If it is in the middle of a housing estate it will probably have to be an inward-looking garden, screened from its neigbours by hedging, with all views inwards. An outward-facing garden makes use of local features such as hills, an attractive church steeple or a specimen tree, making a virtue of it and enhancing the view.

Is the site sloping or flat?
Many people spend an excessive amount of time and money changing the contours of a garden – creating a rock garden on a completely flat site, for instance. It is not only easier, but often just as effective to enhance the natural contours already there.

Is the soil acid or alkaline?
It is well worth the expense to have a soil test done to find out whether the land is acid, alkaline, stony, sandy, clay or whatever. This information is invaluable when choosing the types of plants best suited to the area. Small soil-testing kits are not expensive and are easy to use. This is one area where experience helps. The practised gardener can tell from the plants which are growing well in the neighbourhood, what type of soil predominates.

What is the direction of the prevailing wind?
This again needs to be considered when choosing plants, siting them, and deciding where to put shelter belts to protect the more delicate plants.

What features do you want in the garden?
Again, sit down, study the plan, and make a list. Most people want a lawn. If it is to be the main feature then the other elements should lead off from it – and do not forget the view from the house! A colourful herbaceous or shrub border beyond the lawn is appreciated all the more when it can be viewed from the sitting room. A sunny sitting-out area or patio next to the house leads out on to the rest of the garden. Climbing plants on the house walls provide a colourful and scented entry to the garden – and drifting scent is marvellous when it wafts into the house. Climbing roses are ideal. They look and smell good, and tend to soften the hard features of a wall. There are, of course, many other climbing plants to choose from (see 'Shrubs', Chapter 3). Herbs are both attractive and useful, and need to be close to the kitchen door for easy collection. These days more people prefer to buy rather than grow vegetables – but it is not nearly so much fun! If grown well vegetables are not unsightly things to be hidden away. They can be an added attraction. In fact, it is a mistake to site them too far from the house. Like herbs, they are better close to the kitchen for easy picking in poor weather.

Which prompts the question of paths. Do not leave the vegetable patch, potting shed, or greenhouse stranded without a path. When the grass becomes a quagmire and the soil turns to mud, it is too late to realize the error! In addition a common complaint among housewives is that when designing gardens, husbands never think about a place to hang out the washing! Not that they ever think about the washing until a clean shirt is required – but it is essential to make provision for a line or rotary drier. Dustbins too, need a discreet site, so a little thought at the planning stage can prevent an eyesore later.

Before leaving paths, it pays to remember that straight paths are not a good idea unless the garden has a very formal design. Winding paths are more interesing, more practical, and less demanding. In fact informal gardens are becoming much more popular, and are certainly easier to maintain. They do not show up glaring mistakes as readily as a formal plan, where every line has to be spot-on otherwise it looks awful.

One of the problems with a small plot of land is that most of it can be seen at a glance. If it is possible it is much more interesting to hide certain areas, creating an air of mystery about what is round the corner. Alternatively, draw the eye to a particular feature, such as a statue, in one part of the garden. Or split the site into areas which will provide interest during different seasons of the year.

The plants (or garden furnishings) add colour, form and texture to the basic design, but without proper thought at the design stage, a garden can become just a jumble of plants rather than a living expression of your ideas (Fig. 3).

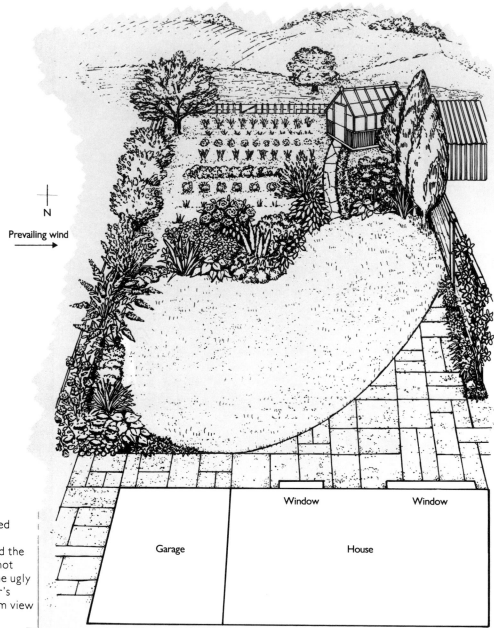

N

Prevailing wind →

Fig. 3 A well-designed garden. Note that a pleasant view beyond the end garden fence is not obscured and that the ugly tin shed in next door's garden is hidden from view by the conifers.

Window   Window

Garage   House

Renovating an established garden

Taking over an established garden presents an entirely different set of problems from those of a new one. There may not be dozens of broken tiles, hundreds of stones, or lumps of concrete to clear – but there could be a jungle of weeds, thorns and ageing shrubs instead.

The best way to tackle an overgrown garden is to tread carefully – and treat it like a neglected rose bush. Dead and diseased material needs to be removed – and this includes trees and shrubs which are past their best, or which will never be specimen plants again. Do not be afraid to dig them up or pull them out. Be ruthless! If the garden is big enough with good access, a tractor and a good strong chain can prove the most useful tools for this heavy work.

Then comes pruning. As with the rose bush this will help give shape and space to breathe. Remove anything which looks untidy, cluttered or an embarrassment to the final design. But be careful. A hedge, which at first sight might only promise extra work, could well turn out to be a necessary and well established windbreak. Hasty removal could set the garden back several years.

Similarly, before removing any other trees or shrubs, take account of their possible value at other times of year, or in future years. They could become an invaluable part of the eventual planting scheme. Gardens which include a few mature trees and shrubs will look established a great deal quicker than those where everything is removed and replanted with new, young growth. If in doubt, leave the plant for a few weeks. Look at it from all angles, from different parts of the house and garden, and at different times of day. Eventually there will be no doubt whether it should stay or go.

2 PATHS AND PATIOS

These are the hard landscaping features as opposed to the 'soft' land-scape of the plants. Blended together they create harmony as well as enabling the garden to 'work' as a construction. But remember, they need to be carefully thought out before being incorporated into the overall design. Paths that lead nowhere are as much use as a back pocket in a vest! Before coming to any decisions make a sketch of the house and garden, then link all those areas that require paths, drives, patio, or some other hard standing area (Fig. 4).

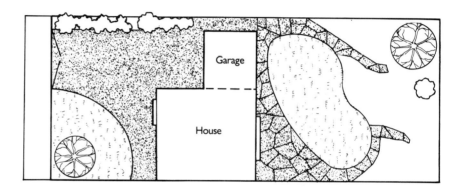

Fig. 4 All paths and drives should be planned first.

Paths and drives

The width, shape and construction of paths should be determined by their purpose. Those that will be used most, like the paths round the house (it's amazing how often the windows need cleaning!) should be more substantial than those that meander through the garden. The materials used should also be in keeping with the period of the house, as well as the layout of the garden. A thatched cottage and comple-mentary garden would definitely not look right with a tarmacadam path.

Make sure all paths are wide enough! It may seem obvious, but as plants sprawl over them, the width will be greatly reduced – perhaps more than you might expect. Pruning back the offending plants will only create a harsh effect. Remember too that plants constantly brushed by a wheelbarrow being trundled up and down a path will be damaged.

If plants are to be grown up the walls of the house – leave a space before laying the paths. This is far easier than making a hole after any concrete has been laid.

Unless the garden design is deliberately formal, try to avoid long straight paths wherever possible. Gentle curves are better.

The same applies to drives. A curved drive, with a turning point for the car, is more aesthetically pleasing, as well as more effective than a straight drive up to the house (Fig. 5). Although the cost of labour and materials for the drive and path in Plan *a* might be slightly less than for the drive in Plan *b*, the difference in effectiveness and pleasing appearance is obvious.

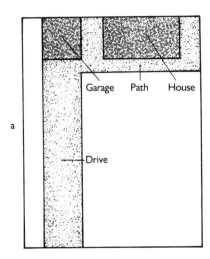
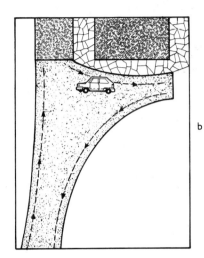

Fig. 5 Careful designing of drives creates a more effective and pleasing result.

Path construction

If you want a solid, hard-wearing path, a certain amount of construction work is necessary before the final surface material can be laid. The area first needs to be marked out accurately with pegs and string. But if a gentle curve is required, a hosepipe laid along the outline will be more effective.

Soil should be removed from the site to a depth of about 23 cm (9 in). Then add 15 cm (6 in) of rubble and firm it in. Follow with a couple of centimetres (about an inch) of fine gravel or sand. (This will make levelling easier before laying the surface material.) These measurements will give you a path capable of withstanding quite heavy machinery. The amounts can be reduced where traffic will be lighter.

Concrete
This is one of the most popular materials. Once laid it will last many years without needing attention and it is relatively easy to lay. Large quantities can be purchased ready mixed, and provided the shuttering (the wooden framework enclosing the path area – see Fig. 6) is in place, the concrete can be poured straight into it. If a curved path is required the boards will have to be bent.

While the concrete is still liquid it should be levelled with a piece of wood known as a 'tamping board' by smoothing out the surface evenly over the whole area. If a non-slip surface is required, the tamping board can be used to make it slightly ribbed. A similar effect can be achieved by lightly dragging a stiff brush over the drying concrete.

Pre-cast slabs or flags
In recent years paving slabs have become more adventurous, being manufactured in various shapes, colours and textures to meet the

Here is an easy way of building attractive, durable steps, with a brick surround filled with cement mortar and surfaced with crazy paving. First excavate the site to the correct levels, using pegs, string and spirit level. Next build the brick surround. Now (*top left*) infill with sufficient cement mortar to bed the broken paving so the slabs finish flush with the top of the brickwork. Level off the slabs with a straight-edge (*top right*). When all the slabs are laid (*below*), leave the mortar to harden for a day or two, then carefully fill the spaces between the slabs, keeping the surface clean.

ever-increasing demand. Path construction is as above, and the slabs are laid by placing a dollop of cement in each corner to help them settle and to stop them rocking on the layer of sand.

Paving stones
Known as 'York' stone, natural stone is justifiably popular though expensive. The natural effect produced enhances a garden far more than artificially coloured concrete. Paving stones can be used as whole slabs or broken up as crazy paving.

The choice of paving materials is almost endless, so note what is used in other gardens and how. The success of any paving material depends on how much wear it is expected to take.

The 'hard' effect of any paths using flags or slabs can be softened by

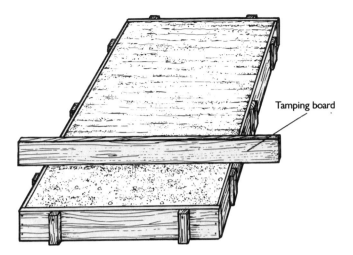

Tamping board

Fig. 6 Tamping board is used to level cement between shuttering.

leaving planting spaces in the surface to grow small specimens, though this method of planting is not recommended on a path that serves as your wheelbarrow's M1!

Chippings
Gravel chippings can form a successful path surface. A note of caution, however: muddy wellies pick up gravel at an alarming rate and transport it wherever the wellies travel! Gravel paths also need an edging to stop the material being washed or kicked on to surrounding borders or lawns. Lawnmowers tend to shout 'Ouch!' in an expensive voice every time they eat chippings.

Logs
Large logs sawn from the main trunk of mature trees make a most effective path with a stepping stone appearance (Fig. 7). They need to be dug in and firmed well. They will last longer if the bark is removed first.

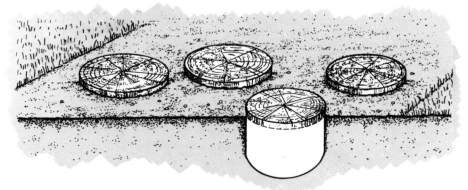

Fig. 7 Logs can be used to create an unusual and hardwearing path.

Pine needles
Where a pine wood is close at hand, and the needles easily and cheaply available, they can be used to great effect in the right setting. Pine needle paths do need an edging to stop the needles escaping, but they are a pleasure to walk on.

Grass

Grass is fine for little-used paths. However, decide to take a wheel-barrow along one in a wet, mild period and your error will be only too apparent. Obviously, it is possible to overcome the problem by using planks, but choosing a more suitable surface at the planning stage will save trouble later.

Chamomile and thyme

Though they are not suitable for heavy wear, and need a great deal of work to keep them weed free, the pleasure gained from treading the length of such paths, or inhaling the scent they give off, makes them a joy.

Remember when planning or constructing any path or drive, it will soon be rained on (the joys of the English climate!) and if water cannot seep through its surface it will form puddles or run down hill (Fig. 8). So make sure the path or drive slopes away from your garage or house or, if this is not possible, incorporate a drain or soakaway at the planning stage – unless, of course, you own an amphibious vehicle.

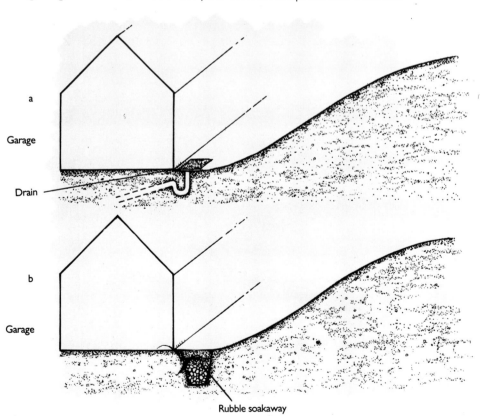

Fig. 8 A drain (*a*) or soakaway (*b*) is essential at the bottom of a sloping drive to prevent the garage flooding.

Patios

Foreign travel has resulted in patios becoming increasingly popular garden features in Britain. It is a pity a warmer climate could not be imported as easily to make the most of them! Nevertheless, a patio can be an attractive and versatile addition to the 'hard' landscape.

Many surfaces can be used, though a smoother surface is generally required than on a path or drive. Stone or concrete slabs are ideal. Gravel is the least suitable as it would be constantly trodden into the house on the soles of shoes. Cobbles are almost as bad. They are not only ankle twisters and the enemy of high heels, but chairs tend to wobble on them, spilling half the gin and tonic!

Size

Make sure the patio is large enough to accommodate people and furniture. While it should be in scale and proportion with the rest of the garden and house, the amount of space required is often underestimated.

Position

Ideally a patio should be sited to take full advantage of the sun for as long a part of the day as possible. Shelter is essential – G and Ts on the patio are fine, goose pimples are not! Wind is not the only consideration. Privacy is important too, particularly if a bit of all-over sunbathing is contemplated!

Design

The styling of the patio must complement and blend in with the house and its surroundings, not be so different that it looks bizarre. These days there is a wide choice of ornamental paving slabs in decorative shapes and colours. Various patterns can be created, but beware of over-ambitious designs – they could turn out to be an eyesore.

Partitioning the patio from the rest of the garden with a low decorative wall enables a separate micro-climate to be created. Careful addition of suitable decoration, urns, pots and certain plants, can create a Mediterranean effect.

With so much 'hard' landscaping involved, it will probably be necessary to soften its appearance with plants. Borders or beds are best as the depth of soil provided will make plants in them less susceptible to drought than their counterparts in tubs or pots.

Trellis can be used to support climbing plants, but a wall involves less maintenance – just a few wires and nails. As many plants take several years to reach maturity, this tends to coincide with the collapse of wooden trellis, or plastic supports becoming brittle. Wires and nails are far easier to replace without disturbing the growing plant.

On the patio itself plants can be grown in tubs, or in the cracks or spaces left in the paving. Again, drying out is less of a problem in the latter. Some plants are a pleasure to walk on, too. Freshly crushed chamomile or thyme is a delight. Occasional, gentle trampling, however, is recommended. The plants will rebel all too obviously if they think a rugby team is making use of them.

A final note of caution: if you're in the habit of walking barefoot on the patio, avoid prickly plants!

3 TREES AND SHRUBS

Trees and shrubs form the skeleton of the garden, dictating its final shape and design. So before planting, or even choosing them, refer back to the original plan. How they are sited is of paramount importance in achieving the best effect, and preventing problems at a later stage. They are also the most expensive plants we grow in the garden and the longest lived. Therefore, buy the best you can afford, then they will reward you with many years of growth and interest.

At the planning stage try to create a balance between deciduous trees and shrubs, and conifers – remembering that conifers tend to create more interest in winter. In Britain we are fortunate that we are able to grow a wide range of shrubs from virtually every country in the world. They generally grow in all types of soil, though plants like rhododendrons and camellias like acid conditions.

The Victorians were fond of shrubberies or shrub borders, but these days it is more fashionable to use shrubs as the skeleton of a mixed border, giving height at the back, filled in with annuals and herbaceous plants.

Trees and shrubs are also useful as windbreaks and partitions. Individual specimens can create focal points of interest in a lawn.

Choosing trees and shrubs

Before even considering going to a nursery or garden centre to select trees, plan carefully what is needed.

When choosing trees to plant, consider the size, colour and texture of their foliage as well as their floral display. You will be looking at their leaves for months, their flowers for but a week or two.

The bark of some trees —
birches are a popular
example — can be highly
ornamental, particularly in
winter after the leaves
have fallen. It is specially
appreciated when the
garden is so bare.

Size

Some trees may take a hundred years to reach their ultimate size, which could be up to 30 m (100 ft) or more. In a suburban garden a tree would be unlikely to occupy its site for that length of time. Therefore, the size it is likely to achieve in 20 years is probably more relevant.

It is impossible to give a precise ultimate height for any tree, however, as so much depends on the condition of the site in which it is growing. If it is warm and sheltered, with good, deep, rich loamy soil, it will do well and grow to its full height. Whereas on a windy, poor site it will not grow as vigorously. The best guide is to go round neighbouring gardens and countryside to see which trees and shrubs are thriving best. If you rely on a catalogue for guidance, remember it can only give a rough estimate of how big a tree or shrub will grow.

Trees are generally divided into three categories: standard, half-standard, and feathered.

Standard:

These are trees with a clear 1.5–1.8 m (5–6 ft) stem. The crown of branches begins above this.

Half-standard

These are, as they suggest, smaller and more suitable for an average to small garden. They only have 1.2–1.5 m (4–5 ft) of clear stem below the branches.

Feathered

These are young trees which have had none of their branches removed, so they extend right down to the base level. They are cheaper than the previous two.

Shape

If space is limited, a fastigiate or columnar tree (which grows straight up rather than spreading outwards) may be best. A little more space would allow a conical or pyramidal shape, or a large round-headed tree. Weeping trees are attractive, but be warned, a weeping willow may grow too large for a small garden.

Foliage

There is a wide variety of foliage to choose from. Some trees have finely divided leaves, others bold or variegated leaves. Attractive shapes, designs and tracery provide variety and interest right through the summer. For autumn colour choose trees such as acers (maples).

Flowers and fruit

Sorbus (mountain ash) provides a wonderful array of flowers in spring and colourful berries in autumn. Hawthorn also produces an abundance of flowers and berries.

Bark

Trees with unusual bark come into their own in winter when peeling or striped (snake) barks are seen at their best. They provide an extra dimension and interest to the garden during the long winter months.

Problems

Before buying any tree consider the damage or nuisance it could cause you or your neighbour in future. If it grows too close to a house or other building it may restrict the amount of light entering. Overhanging branches could cause a hazard, or clog guttering with leaves each autumn.

The wrong choice of tree could cause even more damage underground. Most poplars and some willows take great delight in pushing their roots into drains, and can even undermine house foundations. Paths and drives are easily cracked by their aggressive roots.

Site preparation

If possible, try to prepare the land a few months before planting. This will allow the soil to settle down again. It should be thoroughly cultivated by deep digging, or even ploughing if it is a big area, fertilized with well rotted farmyard manure, and broken down to a good tilth with a fork or rake.

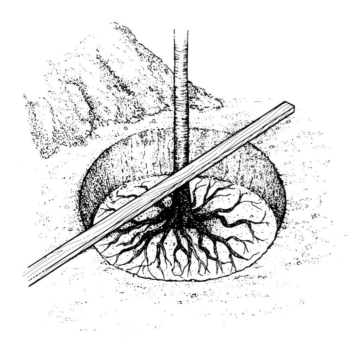

Fig. 9 Planting a tree. Dig a hole big enough to accommodate roots comfortably. Place a piece of wood across the hole to ensure the tree is planted to the same depth as previously.

Plant preparation

The best time to plant trees and shrubs is during winter while they are dormant. If they have been grown in open ground, examine the roots carefully before planting. Remove any dead, broken, damaged or diseased sections. If the roots are dry, soak them in a bucket of water for a couple of hours. Do the same with container-grown plants which may have dried out.

21

The bark of several kinds of maple from the United States is intriguingly marked with longitudinal whitish stripes, like a snake's skin. This snake bark maple is *Acer capillipes*.

A young, six year old *Acer pseudoplatanus* 'Brilliantissimum', glowing with its spectacular spring foliage; a good choice for the small garden.

23

If you receive plants but are not ready to plant them, because of circumstances or weather conditions, dig a hole, lay them on the ground, to prevent them being rocked by the wind, with their roots in the hole, then cover with soil and firm in. This is called 'heeling in', and keeps the roots moist until they are ready for planting.

Soil preparation

The most important thing is to dig a hole big enough for the tree or shrub being planted. If you have spent £10 on a tree, it is worth the effort of digging a £12 hole to give the roots plenty of room.

All trees and shrubs should be planted to the same depth as previously, even if containerized – certainly no deeper. The easiest way to check the depth is to stand the tree in its hole and place a cane across the diameter of the hole. Where the cane crosses the trunk will show whether the depth is correct (Fig. 9).

When digging out the hole, try to keep the top soil and the sub-soil separate. Add peat, general fertilizer, well rotted farmyard manure (fresh manure will scorch the roots) to the soil in the bottom of the hole and fork it in. This will encourage the roots to reach down into the goodness below.

Staking

If a tree can be planted without using a stake it will establish itself quicker than one which relies on support. Stakes tend to make trees lazy. But large trees which have a bigger surface area for the wind to blow and rock around do need staking.

When a stake is needed, set it in the hole at the same time as the tree. Putting it in later could damage the roots. Check the prevailing wind, and place the stake so that the tree blows away from it, not towards it. Blowing on to a stake will damage the tree. However, this may be unavoidable with the branches of thin, whippy trees.

A good stake deserves a good tree tie which will not damage the tree, and will separate the stake and trunk (Fig. 10). Good trees can be ruined if tied with wire or plastic string which will cut into and strangle the trunk. A small piece of hosepipe with string through the centre makes a good tree tie, but commercially made ones are not expensive.

Planting a big specimen tree may need more than just one stake. Three wire guy ropes can be used, protected where they touch the tree. These can be a problem though if there is grass round the tree which requires cutting (Fig. 11).

Planting

Once satisfied that the tree is placed properly in its hole at the correct depth, start replacing the soil, starting with the sub-soil, which could be mixed with peat, well rotted farmyard manure or general fertilizer such as hoof and horn. When filling the hole jiggle the tree about in the replaced soil so that it falls around and fills in any air spaces. Firm down the soil as filling continues with the top soil as it is more evenly compacted. Do not simply replace all the soil and then firm it.

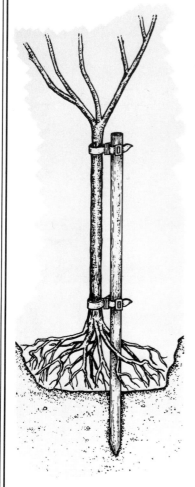

Fig. 10 Insert supporting stake before filling in the hole to avoid damaging the roots. A good tree deserves strong tree ties properly positioned allowing some room for development. The hole must be deep enough to ensure that all roots are below ground level (see Fig. 9, p.21).

If you are planting a large specimen tree, there are two ways of proceeding. Some say that as a large tree will suffer some die-back when it is transplanted, it is better to prune it by up to a third, so that when it starts into growth again in spring it will not have a vast amount of foliage to support. But others maintain that if you buy a tree of a certain size for a special purpose you will not want to reduce it so much. So it is probably better to adopt the second course, planting it in the best possible conditions, followed by good aftercare, then there should be little die-back.

Leave it until spring, then prune anything that has died. A large tree will take longer to re-establish after transplanting than a small one.

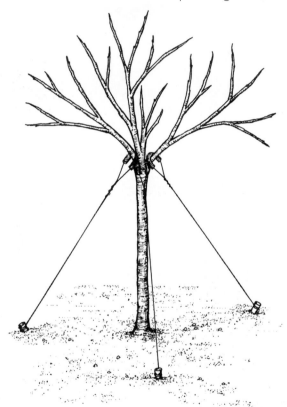

Fig. 11 Guy ropes are an effective way of supporting larger trees.

Shrubs

Shrubs are perhaps the most useful plants available to the gardener. The majority are easy to grow, tolerant of varying soil conditions, and there is a wide range to choose from. They've come a long way since the days of the dowdy Victorian shrubbery, when choice was limited. Thanks to the work of plant hunters and explorers, who brought seeds and plants back to this country from far flung corners of the world, and later to plant breeders, we now have a diversity of plants that would have been the envy of earlier generations of gardeners.

And our climate is ideal. Yes, the wonderful British climate does encourage shrubs to flourish. No wonder gardeners are always blessing the weather!

These days shrubs tend to be used with other groups of plants, such as herbaceous perennials and bulbs, to create spectacular mixed

Many trees, like *Acer negundo* 'Variegata' here, have variegated leaves which serve to enliven the garden scene. But do not overplant such trees or shrubs or your garden will seem restless rather than a place to relax.

A pleasant composition with contrasting green and maroon-leaved trees forming a background to a lower planting of perennials, being admired by the authors.

Conifers deserve a place for their valuable contribution of foliage to the otherwise bare winter garden. Many mature conifers have handsome bark.

27

borders, or as single specimens in lawns. Not only do they enhance the effect of plant groupings by providing a backdrop for them but they also give useful shelter.

Shrubs are so versatile and tolerant, they allow themselves to be subjected to drastic treatment. They can be clipped into hedges, turned into weird and wonderful shapes by the art of topiary, or have their growth stunted by the Japanese bonsai method, which produces miniature trees and shrubs by keeping the roots pruned and confined in containers.

Planting shrubs

Planting shrubs differs little from planting trees. Aim for deep and thorough cultivation of the soil. This is done by 'double-digging', i.e. turning the soil to at least two spade depths. This breaks up the sub-soil and allows the roots to explore and make use of as much volume as possible (Fig. 12).

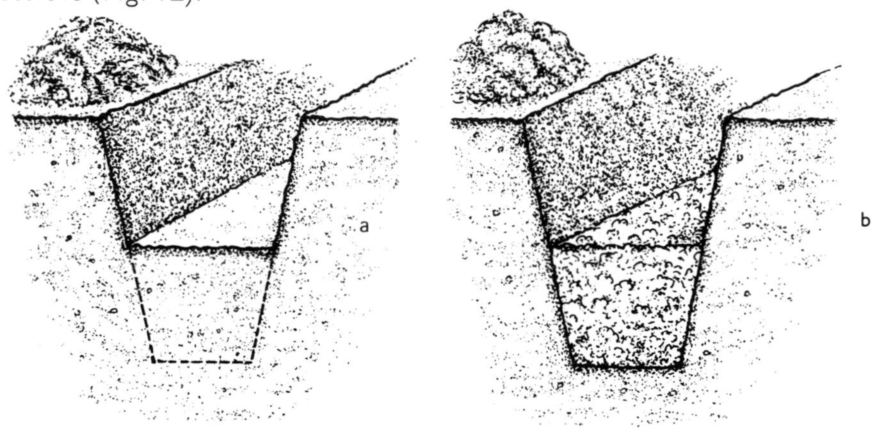

Fig. 12 To enable roots to explore the soil's full potential, deep dig to two spades' depth. (a) Trench dug to one spade's depth, (b) Soil in bottom of trench turned over to another spade's depth.

Though recommended for giving shrubs a good start, double-digging is enough to send gardeners with bad backs or clay soils (often the two go together!) indoors to lie down. After double-digging, the soil should be left for a while to settle down. This also gives the gardener time to recover from his ordeal!

If there is no time for the soil to settle properly before planting, you must tread and rake it to firm it and break down the surface to a reasonable tilth.

Like trees, shrubs need holes dug deep and wide enough to give their roots plenty of room. If the soil is clay, the sides of the hole will tend to glaze as the spade slices through the soil, leaving the shrub in a virtually impenetrable container. This can be overcome by using a fork to tease away the soil and let the roots escape. Do not forget to add some well rotted organic material, such as leaf mould or manure at this stage.

If a shrub is bought 'balled' or 'root-balled', with its roots enclosed in sacking, do remove this before planting as some sacking is slow to rot, or may never rot away. This would eventually lead to the plant being strangled.

Unlike trees, few shrubs need staking. However, it is worthwhile checking during their first year that they are firm in the soil, particularly after spells of windy weather.

There are conflicting views about the ideal distance apart shrubs should be planted. Close planting gives quick results but has the disadvantage that the plants grow into, and spoil, each other. Planting wide enough to allow the shrubs to reach their full size is better in the long term, and meanwhile the gaps can be filled with short-lived shrubs, herbaceous plants or annuals.

Pruning

Most shrubs do perfectly well without pruning. When it is necessary there are a few basic rules:

1. Prune out any dead or diseased wood.

2. Prune out any really old wood – provided this does not totally demolish the shrub.

3. Prune after the flowers have faded, but do not apply this rule for shrubs whose fruits are required. With forsythia and philadelphus, pruning after flowering allows a full season of growth before they flower again.

Spring pruning gives the plants a summer to grow strongly, whereas late summer pruning produces a late flush of soft growth which sometimes cannot harden before winter, and could then succumb to frosts.

Shrubs in the herbaceous border

Shrubs can play a useful role in showing off and sheltering delicate plants. Used among herbaceous plants, shrubs also provide some height and colour in the winter when all their neighbours have died down.

For this reason, evergreens such as *Elaeagnus pungens* 'Maculata' with bright golden variegation are excellent. Winter-flowering shrubs, such as *Viburnum* x *bodnantense* with its scented pink flowers, provide a cheerful splash of colour and interest. Even in summer shrubs can make a border feel established. Plants of elegant habit such as *Sambucus racemosa* 'Plumosa Aurea' (golden-leaved elderberry), or the purple leaves of *Cotinus coggygria* 'Royal Purple' (smoke bush, because of the smoky effect its flowers create), can be a real bonus.

Specimen shrubs and trees

When choosing shrubs to act as specimen plants in lawns, it is customary to choose something unusual but not difficult to mow round. Prickly plants can be a real pain – literally! Plants with a sprawling habit can look untidy.

Some of the acers are magnificent, their foliage a delight. In a sheltered position *Acer palmatum* 'Dissectum Atropurpureum' is lovely, but a little slow to establish.

Amelanchier lamarckii (snowy mespilus) can make a large multi-stemmed shrub which has a haze of white flowers in April/May, and has the added delight of fiery autumn colour.

Many trees are used as lawn specimens. *Acer griseum* (paperbark maple) is a particular favourite. Its rich brown bark which peels so attractively also gives good autumn colour. Though not always readily available, it is a very special garden plant.

The silver birch is popular. One of its forms — *Betula pendula* 'Youngii' — has a weeping habit; *B. pendula* 'Dalecarlica' has cut leaves, while others have pronounced silver white bark, a good form being *Betula utilis*.

Of the flowering crabs, *Malus floribunda* is perhaps the best, flowering April/May. 'Flowering' here is an understatement, as it produces an absolute profusion of blossom, rich rose turning paler with maturity, guaranteed almost every year.

Conifers, with their clean lines, make architecturally pleasing specimens within the garden design. The blue shades of *Chamaecyparis lawsoniana* 'Columnaris Glauca' and the golden *C. lawsoniana* 'Stewartii' are particularly striking.

Hedging shrubs and trees

The choice of hedging plants tends to be an individual matter. In a cottage or country garden exotic species may well look out of place. Beech or hawthorn would probably be better. Privet is over-used. × *Cupressocyparis leylandii* is quick growing — but it keeps on growing . . . and growing, and needs to be kept in check by using secateurs or handshears freely.

There are some attractive forms of berberis, which not only look good, but keep the children and pets in (or out) in the same way as the wonderfully prickly holly.

Climbing shrubs

The range of true climbing shrubs is somewhat limited, but with a little help from trellis or wires that enable them to 'cling', the choice widens.

Parthenocissus henryana is a deciduous climber often called Virginia creeper (along with at least half a dozen other plants) which turns bright red in autumn.

Eccremocarpus scaber is virtually herbaceous, often dying back to ground level each winter, but shooting 2–2½ m (6–8 ft) during the summer. A little protection around the base is appreciated in winter. The flowers, from early summer onwards, are tubular and can be red, orange or yellow depending on type. They are a little different from the more commonly chosen clematis.

Wisteria is an admirable plant. Flowers appear in long racemes (pendulous clusters) in May, and even in the North (in a good summer) a small second flush of flowers can be expected.

The dark evergreen *Garrya elliptica* has graceful catkins and is a useful plant for the darker wall.

When choosing climbers take advantage of the fact that their climbing habit means they are striving to get nearer our noses! So remember to plant some near your doors and windows so the heavenly scent from their flowers can waft into the house. Some of the fragrant honeysuckles are ideal.

LAWNS

A lawn is a marvellous feature in a garden. It can be the dominant feature without appearing to be, by leading the eye into the borders and other areas of interest.

It is a mistake though, to assume that if the garden is put down to lawn, it need only be mown once a week or fortnight, and that is the end of it. Effort is required to create a good lawn – but it is worth it!

Creating a lawn

Few people give enough thought to the lawn's aspect, or to the type and fertility of the soil on which it is grown. When creating a lawn think of it as a collection of grass plants, which is what it is.

Aspect

Grass plants prefer an open aspect, they need plenty of light, and wind across the foliage, as air movement prevents fungal diseases developing.

Soil types

A slightly acid soil is best for most grass plants, so before sowing seed a soil test is advisable. If it is too alkaline flowers of sulphur can be applied to make it more acid, and if too acid use lime to bring it back to pH 6.5. The depth of soil and underlying rock may determine how often these are applied.

If conditions are right from the start, the plants will have a better chance of survival if things turn against them later. The establishing factors are most important in the life of any garden plant.

Fertility

Opinions vary greatly over how much fertilizer lawns require. Fertilizer manufacturers tend to recommend 60 g per sq m (2 oz per sq yd), whereas 30 g per sq m (1 oz per sq yd) is usually quite adequate. Grass does not actually need a lot of goodness in the soil to grow well. In fact the best 'lawns' are often those grazed by sheep which fertilize the ground naturally.

But it must be remembered that when lawn clippings are removed by mowing, goodness is removed which must be replaced. Less goodness is removed by mowing frequently, just taking the tips off the grass, than by leaving it for a couple of weeks when a much greater length will need removing.

Drainage

This is a vital consideration before seed sowing or laying turf. Grass seeds prefer well drained soil. On sandier soils, for example, they grow much further down and develop a better root system than on clay. If the lawn is going to be subject to wear, such as heavy use by children, a good root system is essential, so on badly drained land it is worthwhile putting in a drainage system before doing anything else.

The most important thing to decide before laying a drainage system is where the outlet is to be situated. Start there, and work back into the middle, otherwise it may not work (Fig. 13). Contractors will do the job for you, but it is relatively simple to lay a drainage system in the average garden. Clay pipes, land tiles and plastic pipes are cheap, all are readily available, and the plastic ones are very easy to install.

Different grasses

Different types of grass are needed for making a bowling green on the one hand, and a lawn that is to take a lot of wear on the other. Also grass comes in widely varying shades of green, which can alter according to weather and soil conditions. At some times of the year it can look positively yellow.

When it comes to choosing grass seed, a wide range is available these days. A high quality lawn can be created by using a mixture of 80% Chewings fescue and 20% Brown top bent, whereas a lawn that will stand plenty of hard wear needs a mixture containing perennial rye grass.

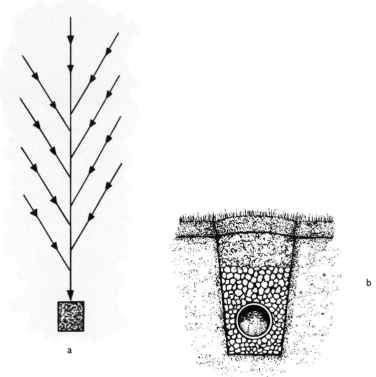

Fig. 13 Drainage: (a) a herringbone system is an effective method of drainage; (b) laying the pipes in gravel further improves the effectiveness of the drain.

Science has helped vastly to improve grass types. For instance, the clever boffins at Aberystwyth University came up with a variety called S23, which is dwarfer flowering and leafier than traditional grasses. This overcomes the problem of grass which when mown is pushed over by the mower and leaves behind a nasty flower stalk and 'feathers'. More recent introductions have even superseded this super seed!

Grass mixtures

Dwarf perennial rye is excellent for lawns, but a mixture is better because, if pests or disease attacks a specific grass it can ruin the whole lawn. A mixture will reduce that risk. A lawn also needs a mixture of bottom, or low grasses like Brown top bent, and higher ones such as Chewings fescue. Another advantage of a mixture is that some seed types germinate much more quickly than others, and act as a nurse to the slower growing ones.

Quality mixture
> 7 parts Chewings fescue
> 3 parts Brown top bent

Utility mixture
> 4 parts Chewings fescue
> 3 parts perennial rye grass
> 2 parts crested dogs tail
> I part rough-stalked meadow grass

Shade tolerant mixture
> 5 parts rough-stalked meadow grass
> 3 parts wood meadow grass (*Poa nemoralis*)
> 2 parts creeping red fescue

Soil preparation

Preparing the surface for grass depends on whether it is to be seeded or turfed. A finer finish is needed for seeds, though preparation is very similar.

If it is a large area, it can be ploughed, cultivated and harrowed. If it is a small patch, dig it, then rake and tread it. (Treading is the strange activity where you walk up and down firming the soil with your heels like a penguin . . . first making sure the neighbours are not watching!)

Before starting to dig, make sure there are no major pests or disease problems. This is unlikely unless the land has been pasture for many years, when it would be as well to put down some pesticide (see Pests and Diseases).

Weeds tend to be the biggest problem at this stage. If the soil is full of annual weeds – those which grow, flower and seed in one year – there is no need to worry unduly, because most of them will die out with constant mowing. It is the perennials with long tap roots, sometimes 60–90 cm (2–3 ft) long, that have to be eradicated. Mowing will not kill them, but weedkiller will.

If you are reluctant to use weedkiller, and time is not a problem, the ground can be left fallow for a year. Just keep hoeing the weeds. If this is done often enough throughout the growing season, perennial weeds will be so weakened that they will eventually die off. But it does take a full season and a lot of hard work.

Many people make the mistake of levelling a big expanse of soil for their lawn. Unless you are creating a formal effect do not level the land. A gently rolling lawn with sloping gradients and different levels looks far more natural. But it is important to make sure the surface is true, with all the bumps taken out, so that it can be mown easily.

Where the garden belongs to a new house it is likely to be full of rubble and big stones, which must be cleared, but if the land contains only very small stones, these can later be rolled beneath the surface.

Sowing grass seed

It takes a lot of hard work to prepare the soil properly for grass seed, but the effort will be repaid later when the lawn matures. Raking and treading finds all the hollows and soft spots, and, if done thoroughly will make sure the lawn's foundation is equally firm all over.

Time of year to sow

The best time to sow grass seed is in August or September. This gives the grasses a chance to get established before winter frosts set in. You can sow in spring, but this is second best as it does not give the grasses time to grow sufficiently to withstand summer droughts. (Yes, we do occasionally have long, hot summers!)

Timely tip

Having chosen the most suitable grass mixture for the conditions and type of lawn you want, give the container of seeds a good shake before you do anything else. Seeds are different shapes and sizes, and during storage and carriage all the small seeds will have sunk to the bottom, leaving the bigger ones on top. Sowing straight from an unshaken packet could result in a peculiar lawn with all the big grass seeds at one end, and the small ones at the other, which obviously defeats the object of a mixture.

Quantities

Approximately 50 g of grass seed per sq m ($1\frac{1}{2}$ oz per sq yd) is generally regarded as the optimum distribution.

To see what this looks like, mark out a square metre (or yard), weigh out the amount of seed required and scatter it evenly over the square.

Sowing

Divide the amount of grass seed required for the entire lawn into two equal parts. Sow one part up and down the lawn area. Then sow the other across. This gives a more even sowing and avoids any bald patches (in the new lawn.)

Most domestic lawns are small enough to sow by hand, but mechanical seed distributors can be hired from seed merchants or garden centres. After sowing, rake the soil surface lightly if it is not too wet, and go over the surface with a light roller. This will help to put the seed and soil in better contact and help to promote quicker germination. Then just wait for Mother Nature to take her course.

Opposite: A well-kept lawn is the almost indispensable centrepiece of most gardens, setting off the flower borders splendidly, its cool relaxing green contrasting with the flowers' often strident colours.

Rolling and mowing

Once the seeds have germinated, but before it is ever mown, go over it again with a light roller. At this stage the grasses should be about 4 cm (1½ in) long.

The roller on a cylinder mower is ideal for this purpose as it is not too heavy. (Remember to knock the cutting blade out of action, or hold the handles down to lift the front blades off the ground). Rolling at this stage will push any small stones down under the surface out of the way of the cutting blades.

More importantly, rolling bends the blades of grass making the lawn tiller (If you have visions of Tiller girls, don't get too excited!) It means that when bent the leaf stops growing and forces the grass plant to send up two leaves from down below – the same principle as in pruning.

Two or three days later the grass will stand up again, ready for its first hair cut! Set the mower blades high enough just to take the tips off, and make sure the blades are very sharp so they cut cleanly and do not tear the new grasses (see Lawn mowers p 39). Cylinder mowers create a better lawn than rotary machines. Their scissors action gives a clean, tidy cut, whereas the rotary action tends to tear the leaves, leaving them jagged and more susceptible to fungal diseases.

After care

As the lawn develops, mow it regularly, gradually bringing down the height of cut to 2 cm (¾ in) for a good quality lawn, and 3 cm (1¼ in) for a utility lawn. Remove any annual weeds, and any perennial ones that escaped the initial weed killing.

During the lawn's first season take care that it does not dry out. If it starts to, give it a really good soaking, so the water saturates at least 10 cm (4 in) down. Using a sprinkler for only ten minutes will do more harm than good as it will encourage the grass roots to come up towards the surface where the only moisture is.

Annual care

September: increase the intervals between mowing.

October: raise the height of cut for the last few mowings and scarify (raking out the dead grasses which form a mat). Also spike the lawn and add top dressing.

November: worm killing—or preferably, discouraging, if necessary. Generally worms do more good than harm, so only take action where wormcasts are a serious problem.

December, January, February: keep off the lawn, particularly in frosty weather when walking on it will leave brown footmarks. It will not kill the lawn, but it looks unsightly.

March: vigorous brushing removes rubbish that has accumulated. A light rolling and mowing just to top the grass will give it a good start into the new growing season.

April: treat any moss that has developed.

May: weedkilling and mowing.

June, July: normal summer mowing. If there's a drought, raise the height of the cut.

August: spot-treat any weeds which have survived the major weed-killing in May.

Grass in shady areas

Grass may not grow well under trees, or in the shade of a house or other building. However, *Poa nemoralis*, commonly known as wood meadow grass, copes well with shady conditions.

Seed versus turf

A lawn grown from seed is the cheapest and easiest. It enables you to sow exactly the mixture you require (and as a result of EEC regulations you can now guarantee that the seed you order is the correct mix).

It is now possible to buy turf made up to the mixture you need from specialist firms who sow the seed mixture and then sell it as turf, but this is expensive. However, if you need to create a small lawn quickly, it might be worth while.

Another problem with turf is that you never know where it has been! How often 'top quality' turf is advertised in local newspapers, which turns out to be farmer Brown's field that has been mown a couple of times, lifted along with all the weeds and cow pats, and for which the customer is charged the earth!

Laying turf

Turf is usually bought in rolls or squares, and is quite easy to lay as long as a few basic rules are followed.

Fig. 14 Laying turf (*a*) Working from a plank protects the turfs already laid and the prepared soil surface.

The most important is to start laying turf from the outside of the lawn area and work inwards. This is because the edges get all the wear and tear and dry out the quickest, and because it is easier to fill in the awkward shapes that are left if they are in the middle.

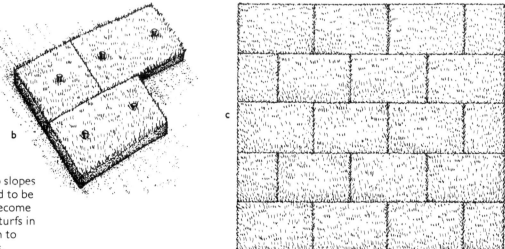

Fig. 14 (*b*) On steep slopes some turfs may need to be pegged until they become established. (*c*) Lay turfs in a brickwork pattern to strengthen the joins.

Always use the largest turfs on the outside, and fill in the middle with half-turfs, quarter-turfs and all the odd shapes that are left over. They will be protected by the surrounding regular turfs.

To avoid damaging the turf while it is being laid, stand on a board. Lay the first row of turf along the outside edge, then lay a long wide plank over them, and stand on this to lay the next row.

Push or butt the turfs tightly together, so there are no gaps to let air in and dry them out. Lay them in a brickwork pattern as if building the wall of a house. This spreads the joins out evenly along the whole surface (Fig. 14).

When all the turfs are laid, top dress with dry, sterilized loam (i.e. loam without any weed seeds), sand or peat—or even a mixture of all three. This improves the soil and fills in all the cracks. Use at least 0.5 kg (1 lb) of general top dressing per sq m (yd). Apply this to the surface of the turf and then work it briskly with a brush round the base of the grass plants, levelling off any minor undulations and filling in cracks. Don't leave any dressing on the foliage as this could encourage fungal diseases.

Turfing in autumn or winter – when weather conditions allow – helps to avoid drying out problems. People and animals will be less likely to use the new turf during the winter too.

In spring, though, it is vital not to let the turf dry out. If it does the squares will shrink, and the corners will curl up and twist. No matter how much water is applied after this, the turf will not swell again, so it is important to irrigate the surface at the first sign of drying out.

If turfing a steep bank (seeds would tend to wash away), put one or two wooden pegs through the turfs to hold them in place.

To sow grass seed evenly it helps if you mark out a square yard of prepared ground with canes and string and sow the prescribed 1½ oz. of seed over it to gauge how thickly to sow it.

Lawn mowers

You can't beat a cylinder mower for creating and maintaining a really good quality lawn. Not only is its clean, efficient scissor action far better for the grass plants (see Rolling and mowing p 36), but the front and rear rollers give the lawn a light roll every time the grass is mown. The grass box is also a great advantage as it prevents cut grass going back on to the lawn to die and produce a thatch at the base of the plants. More important still, if the lawn has a weed problem the seeds are not re-introduced, as the flower heads and weed seed are thrown into the collection box.

Rotary mowers have improved tremendously in their grass collection in recent years, but the cut still does not match that of a cylinder mower. The major advantage of a rotary mower is that it can tackle longer grass if for any reason the lawn is not cut for a while, e.g. if you go away on holiday and a friendly neighbour forgets to mow your lawn as promised!

How often should grass be cut?

There is no hard and fast rule. For a really good lawn it should be cut as often as possible – but, more practically, whenever there is time. An interval of eight or nine days gives a reasonable finish, but you need to cut it twice a week for an immaculate lawn.

Before unleashing a cylinder mower on any lawn it should be properly set up, with the cut level on both sides of the blade section (Fig. 15).

Fig. 15 The height at which your cylinder mower cuts can be judged by placing a board on the two rollers and measuring the distance between the bottom of the board and the fixed metal cutting plate. Ensure a level cut by measuring at both ends of the rollers.

Many people make the mistake of always mowing the lawn in the same direction. This is not a good practice, as the grass plants then always lie the same way which exaggerates hollows. It is far better to mow in a different direction each week. This helps to even out the hollows, and at the end of the season, when top dressing is necessary, it will be easier to find any deviations in level.

Rolling the lawn

So-called experts always want to roll grass, whether on lawns or playing fields. In fact, grass rarely needs a heavy roller on it. The only place where heavy rolling is an advantage is on a cricket wicket – which is because cricketers do not really want grass! They need a bone hard surface, very much like a piece of concrete. All the grass is shaved off, the soil is compacted and the roots suffer. After a cricket match a great deal of renovation work is necessary to remove compaction and restore drainage and air movement to allow the roots to breathe again.

The roller on a cylinder mower is quite heavy enough for lawns. A roller is only useful in spring after winter frosts have lifted the turf, or on a new lawn.

It is a fallacy that a roller will even out all the lumps and bumps on a lawn. A heavy roller may squash down a slightly bumpy surface, but it will sink into hollows and make them worse. A roller causes compaction and reduces surface drainage, so it does more harm than good to a lawn.

Weeds and weedkillers

A weed has been described as a plant growing where we do not want it to grow. Most annual weeds will disappear with frequent mowing, but perennial weeds – those with long tap roots such as thistles and dandelions – are more of a problem.

If the soil has been thoroughly prepared, the perennial weeds should have been removed. But if some remain, it is well worth going round hand weeding (provided the area is not too large). There are small weed grubbers which get underneath perennial weeds, pulling them out along with the whole root. But be careful not to break the tap root or a new young plant will grow up again from that point.

On a large area, or where weeds have not been previously removed, the chemical weedkillers may be the only answer.

Selective weedkillers

These can be selective in a variety of ways. The vast majority of weed-killers used on lawns today are hormone weedkillers (e.g. 2,4-D and MCPA, abbreviations for long chemical names), which are safe to use on established lawns, but not on new ones.

They work by making the weeds outgrow themselves in the same way that fertilizer boosts plant growth, but to an exaggerated level, so that the weeds literally grow themselves to death! They are best applied in spring when both grass and weeds are growing strongly. As the grass plants are growing vigorously too they will help to fill in the spaces left by the dying weeds. If the spaces are not filled in quickly, more weed seeds will rush in and germinate.

Most lawn weedkillers are available in spray form, but great care must be taken not to allow the spray to drift on to the plants in sur-rounding beds and borders or they too will outgrow themselves and die. It is very easy to get spray drift on the rest of the garden, so proper precautions are essential.

  (a) always read the manufacturer's instructions on the side of the container.
  (b) never spray when it is windy.
  (c) always get the nozzle as near to the ground as possible while maintaining proper cover with the weedkiller.

To overcome the problem of spray drift, several manufacturers now offer weedkillers in granular form. These can be applied like fertilizers by hand or applicator. Others make a fertilizer and weedkiller combined in granular form, which not only boosts the growth of the grass, but kills the weeds at the same time. Although this seems a neat and easy way of applying the two, it is an expensive way of using chemicals, and is really only worthwhile on small areas.

Lawn sands have a caustic action. They burn the weeds and spare the grasses – but they are expensive.

Growth retardants

For the reluctant gardener, or for controlling grass in places awkward to reach with a mower, e.g. grassy banks, use a chemical growth retar-dant, which slows down the growth of the grass. One of the first of these to come on the market was Maleic hydrazide. This and other

41

similar products are only suitable for rough grass. Certainly not for fine lawns – they deserve time and effort!

Pests

Earthworms
It may seem strange to class earthworms as pests as they generally do such a good job in the garden, burrowing into the soil, aerating it, and helping drainage. They also effectively dig the soil by moving earth and humus about. However, wormcasts can be a problem and an irritation on lawns. They look unsightly. When the lawnmower goes over them they make a muddy mark and they also provide an ideal site for weed seeds to germinate.

So it is really the casts and not the worms which need to be eradicated. Out of the 25 species of worm in Great Britain, only three actually make casts. They are *Allolobophora nocturnas, Allolobophora terrestris* and *Lumbricus terrestris*. There are chemicals on the market which kill worms, but as they do so much good in the garden it would be a great pity to do this. There are other products which just deter them and encourage them to move elsewhere.

Removing wormcasts
Cylinder lawnmowers can be fitted with brush and comb sets which help remove casts tidily. The brush is easily attached in front of the front roller, and as it moves over the lawn it tickles the surface of the grass and breaks down the wormcasts, which in summer dry out very quickly and so do not leave a muddy smear. A metal comb can be fixed between the front roller and the cylinder. This lightly scarifies the grass before it is cut, and helps revitalize the lawn surface.

Leatherjackets (Tipula paludosa)
These are the grubs of the crane fly or Daddy-long-legs. It is not always apparent that they are attacking the lawn, as they nibble away at the roots beneath the surface. The best indication of their presence is hoards of starlings swooping down, pecking and tearing at the turf in search of the grubs. They make more of a mess than the insects themselves! Most soil insecticides will get rid of leatherjackets.

Diseases

Fusarium nivale (snow mould)
As the name suggests, this creates a white mould on the surface of the affected area, causing little circles of diseased-looking turf. If not treated it will eventually kill the grass. It is most common on lawns which are over-fed, and is most prevalent in shaded, damp conditions in autumn and winter.

As with all fungal diseases prevention is better than cure. A systemic fungicide such as Benomyl should be used during the growing season when the chemical will be translocated throughout the plant's vascular system. In winter use a contact fungicide such as quintozene.

Corticium (red thread)

This produces little hairy fungus tentacles on individual blades of grass. It can be detected most easily if the grass is inspected closely early in the morning. Most fungal diseases develop on soft, lush growth, but this one occurs on grass which is struggling and undernourished. It is most prevalent in summer, and is a disease which puts the lawn under stress rather than killing it.

The only treatment necessary is a feed of low nitrogen fertilizer to give it a boost.

Moss in lawns

There are chemicals which kill moss, but it will return if the conditions which first caused it are not tackled effectively. There are always good reasons for moss developing:

(a) if the soil surface is over compacted, which stops air circulating in the ground.

(b) if the pH (acidity) of the soil is too high or too low.

(c) poor drainage.

(d) if old grass has not been removed, so it forms a thatch which provides an excellent home for moss.

(e) the lawn is in deep shade.

(f) the lawn has been scalped. Patches of grass and surface soil have been shaved off by the lawnmower's blades being set too low.

Find out which of these applies and try to improve it if possible Then go round with a moss killer, usually based on lawn sand or mercury compounds.

5 ROSES

Roses play an important role in the garden, historically as well as aesthetically. Monks were probably the first people to cultivate roses, for medicinal purposes and for use in religious ceremonies.

Over the centuries wild species roses have been collected and cross pollinated to produce the wide selection of roses we have today. The vast selection of new varieties have added their own beauty and character to our gardens.

Old roses

The first roses to be introduced from the wild were the bush roses now known as old roses. They have a shorter blooming season and are more susceptible to disease than the modern varieties, but for many people their charm and romance outweigh these disadvantages.

Modern roses

These are the large flowered (formerly hybrid teas) and cluster-flowered roses (floribundas). These roses are shorter, more brightly coloured, more disease resistant, and flower longer than the old roses.

When creating a new variety, rose breeders try to breed such desirable characteristics as fine colour, scent and disease resistance into it.

Propagation

Large-flowered and cluster-flowered roses are usually propagated by budding. A bud of the desired variety is taken from an existing plant and inserted into a T-shaped cut in a rootstock. Rootstocks are really wild roses, or their selected forms, with more vigorous roots than modern roses. The most common rootstock is *Rosa laxa*.

Roses grown on such rootstocks establish much more quickly and vigorously than those grown on their own roots. But a disadvantage of rootstocks is that some are prone to suckering (producing their own characteristic shoots from the roots). If suckers do appear, don't just cut them off. This would have the same effect as pruning and produce more and stronger suckers. Remove as much soil as possible from around the base of the plant and tear away the sucker where it joins the root.

Choosing roses

The best way to choose roses is to see them growing in a nursery or a garden. You can then see straightaway how the varieties compare — which are doing well and which are victims to pests and diseases. If you cannot do this, catalogues are a great help, but there is really no substitute for seeing the plants for yourself.

Many nurseries and garden centres allow customers to label the roses they have chosen to make sure they get those specific plants when they are lifted in autumn. Always select one with at least two strong, healthy main stems, at least the thickness of a pencil (Fig. 16).

Beware of cheap offers advertised in newspapers and magazines. Remember that you only get what you pay for – cheap offers usually mean cheap and nasty roses!

Roses are sold in a variety of ways:

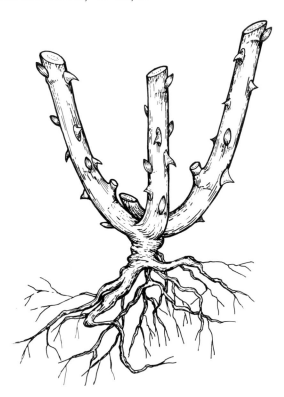

Fig. 16 A healthy rose bush has a strong root system and at least two vigorous stems.

Bare rooted
This is the traditional way of selling roses, and the cheapest. They are lifted without any soil clinging to the roots, put in a bag and sold. The disadvantages are that they can only be bought and planted during the winter, and their roots could dry out, particularly if they are sent through the post. If they have dried out, soak them for at least two hours in a bucket of water.

One great advantage of buying bare-rooted plants is that you can see immediately if there is any damage to the roots.

Container grown
These are grown in their own individual containers. They are more expensive as they cost more to produce, but they are available throughout the year and can be planted at any time.

When buying in the summer do not be tempted by plants carrying two or three attractive flowers. Look beneath the flowers and make sure the plant is healthy and sturdy. Do not be fooled by a bit of colour.

Above: The strangely attractive striped flower of the old rose 'Rosa Mundi', correctly known as *Rosa gallica* 'Versicolor'.

Below: 'Rosa Mundi', as you can see, is generous with its flowers. A row of bushes could form an eye-catching garden divider.

Above: The magnificent semi-double quartered flower of 'Henri Martin', a moss rose, so called after the mossy glands on the sepals behind the flower.

Below: 'Glenfiddich', a cluster-flowered or floribunda rose, is a most distinctive and unusual golden amber.

Containerized
These plants masquerade as container-grown roses, but have been raised as bare-rooted plants and planted in containers later. Consequently they are neither as good nor as versatile as container-grown plants.

Pre-packed
These are sold mainly in supermarkets in polythene bags with a pretty picture on the front. They are produced cheaply, but are not as good as container-grown plants. If they have been sitting in a warm shop for several weeks, or even months, they may have dried out or even started into growth.

Planting

Perhaps the most important thing to remember when planting roses – or any tree or shrub for that matter – is to dig a hole big enough to take its roots comfortably without cramping. It is silly to buy a plant for £1 and put it in a 50p hole!

Time of year
Whatever form of rose you buy, the best time for planting is during the dormant season, preferably late autumn, so its roots can become well established before winter takes hold. Any time during the winter is suitable provided the ground is not too wet. Just use your common sense. Make sure the roots and any soil around them have not dried out. If necessary soak them well for a couple of hours in a bucket of water. No amount of watering later will persuade dried-out roots to grow again!

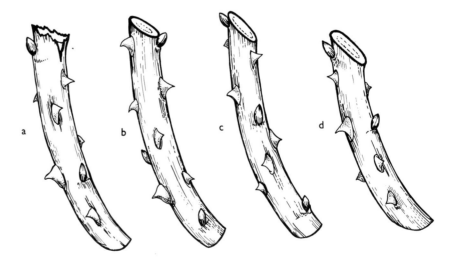

Fig. 17 Pruning roses (*a*) A jagged cut encourages disease and rotting. (*b*) A sloping cut towards the bud directs water and fungal spores on to it. (*c*) Here the cut is too close to the bud. (*d*) A correct cut.

Pruning before planting
Reduce the height of the branches to stop the plant blowing about in the wind, and cut out any dead material. If the roots are thin, wispy or damaged. trim them slightly to make them bush out.

Care of roses

In spring prune roses hard back. The harder the rose is pruned the better it will respond with new growth.

During the first year, when the plants are getting established, make sure they do not dry out, being particularly vigilant during times of drought.

A mulch of leaf mould, peat or spent hops will help conserve moisture, as well as keeping down weeds. In fact mulching and the use of chemical weedkillers is a better way to control weeds around roses than hoeing. Hoeing between roses risks catching and damaging the roots, which encourage suckers to develop from the points of injury.

Disbudding

This technique is only for the enthusiast and used to produce fewer but bigger blooms for showing.

Pests and diseases

Pests

The most common pests of roses are greenfly or aphids, which breed by the thousand. They rapidly swarm over young shoots and emerging buds, sucking out the sap and distorting young foliage and buds. The best treatment is to use a systemic insecticide.

Diseases

Mildew is the most common. The best treatment is to prevent it by spraying with a fungicide. Some sprays contain insecticide and fungicide, so they can get rid of pests and diseases at the same time.

Black spot and *rust* attack the leaves, and are immediately obvious. Any affected leaves should be removed and burnt. Chemicals are available, but they are not entirely effective at containing the disease. Keeping the plants healthy by good husbandry is more effective, using the chemicals to prevent rather than cure an outbreak.

6 HERBACEOUS PLANTS AND BULBS

Fashion not only changes the way *we* look, but also the appearance of our gardens, and the herbaceous plants have borne the brunt of changing fashions.

In the past, no garden was complete without its herbaceous border – such a colourful asset during the summer months. Often backed by a hedge, with the tallest plants grading down to the smaller kinds at the front, leading the eye out on to the lawn. But the amount of work involved in tying and staking the taller plants made gardeners look for more labour-saving ideas.

However, the fall from grace was short-lived. Thanks to science and the plant breeders smaller varieties of old favourites were developed and herbaceous plants have enjoyed a revival. They are now easier to grow than their forebears and tend to be more resistant to disease.

But the old-fashioned herbaceous border has tended to be superseded by the more versatile island bed cut out of the lawn (Fig. 18). This can be viewed from all round, so the taller plants now occupy the centre of the bed, with the smaller ones grading down towards the perimeter. An island bed not only has the advantage of interest from all angles, but its shape becomes a key part of the garden design.

Herbaceous plants are also widely used in mixed borders, adding softness and colour to the harsher lines of the shrubs.

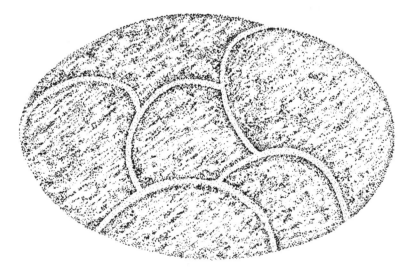

Fig. 18 An island bed marked out with sand to designate different planting areas – see also photograph opposite.

Herbaceous plants embrace a larger range of plants than might at first be imagined. This somewhat misleading description encompasses 'hardy perennials', most of which die down to ground level in winter to grow and flower again each summer, and plants like *Stachys lanata* (lamb's lugs) which retain their leaves throughout the winter.

Marking prepared ground with a trickle of sand provides a useful guide for accurate planting or sowing of flower beds or borders.

Herbaceous plants build up into clumps which need lifting and dividing every three to four years. This makes them extremely useful and economical plants, as propagation costs nothing more than a little effort!

Planning the herbaceous border

Even after the most careful planning and thorough ground preparation, a site can still be dry or wet, cold or warm, windy or calm — and so the site is often the deciding factor when choosing plants. Attention to detail is essential. Herbaceous plants range from those which withstand considerable drought to those which prefer a positively soggy site. But most prefer a sunny site with a fertile, moisture-retentive soil with a pH of around 6.5. (pH is a measure of soil acidity/alkalinity, shown on a scale of numbers up to 14 with 7 as neutral. Low numbers indicate acid soils, higher numbers, above 7, show alkaline soils.) Most plants prefer neutral to slightly acid soils.

If the soil is very wet, it may be necessary to lay land drains. If it is too dry, adding bulky organic material such as manure, spent hops or peat to the soil will help hold some moisture, as will mulching the surface of the soil. A mulch will also help discourage weeds!!

Another way to ease the problem of drought is to lay a drainpipe at the start — not to drain away excess water, but, connected to a tap, to bring water to root level rather than the surface where it will evaporate in the summer warmth.

Moisture-loving plants

The list of herbaceous plants is vast. The following are just a few suggestions to start a collection.

Astilbes
These lovely plants have delicate and attractive foliage. There is a whole range of named varieties with flowers in the red–pink–white range. Although these plume-flowered plants are mostly 60–90 cm (2–3ft) tall they can be as small as 30 cm (12 in) including their flower spikes, like *Astilbe chinensis pumila*, or as tall as 1.5 m (5 ft) like *Astilbe tacquetii superba*.

Rodgersias
These are noble waterside plants. Their foliage, often horse-chestnut-shaped, sets off their own flowers and those of neighbouring plants. The flowers are pink/cream or white depending on species.

Trollius
The globe flowers look like large buttercups, which is what they are. Nodding golden heads compement their rich, green leaves. Most of this group will reach 60–75 cm (2–2½ ft). The luxuriant appearance of the foliage is an indication that these plants appreciate a nutrient-rich soil.

Plants for dry soils

Anaphalis triplinervis

A most popular, though not spectacular plant, extremely reliable and a useful foil for other plants. It has grey-green foliage with creamy white 'everlasting' flowers in late summer. With a height of 30 cm (12 in) it is a popular front of the border plant.

Stachys lanata

Commonly called 'lamb's lugs' this is a favourite with children of all ages! Its soft velvety foliage is a delight to touch, and the silver-grey leaves form a luxuriant carpet. The variety 'Silver Carpet' is non-flowering, but the species bears spikes of pink-purple flowers.

Sedum spectabile

Another plant for the front of the border, a little over 30 cm (12 cm) in height. The variety 'Autumn Joy' has large plate-like flower heads in shades of pink, and is justifiably popular. Its name tells us when it entertains us — and also countless bees and butterflies.

A strange characteristic of gardeners is that they spend the summer spraying caterpillars, then in autumn take great delight in every butterfly that passes, except the Cabbage White!

Plants for average soils

There is a wide range of really beautiful herbaceous plants that thrive in the average border soil.

Chrysanthemums

The species *Chrysanthemum maximum* offers some splendid varieties. 'Wirral Supreme', a double with yellow-centred white flowers is a great favourite. A most reliable plant, it is a real asset to any garden.

Delphinium

The delphinium probably typifies the image of the herbaceous border more than any other plant. Its magnificent flower spikes can reach 2.1 m (7 ft) in height.

Though the merit of a well-grown delphinium has never been questioned it takes a lot of hard work, mulching, staking, tying, and combating that old enemy the slug, to produce the expected magnificence.

Easier to manage dwarf varieties have been developed in recent years, and are now more popular than their more stately forebears.

Although mainly in shades of blue, there are also white and pinky-blue delphiniums and work is still continuing to produce a good quality red.

Hostas

No selection of herbaceous plants would be complete without these noble plants. Though not traditional herbaceous border plants, they have come to the fore among perennials because of their admirable foliage and form.

Some need a little shade and all appreciate a moist soil. Provide these conditions and they will repay you handsomely.

Unfortunately, they are another delicacy of those miserable molluscs, the slugs, which if not kept at bay will quickly shred a large, bold leaf into a quivering doyley.

Grown more for their foliage than their flowers, hostas range from kinds with large, heavily veined rounded leaves to small, slim, elegant specimens with delicate variegations and edgings to the leaves. Most yield mauve flower spikes about 30–60 cm (1–2 ft) in late summer.

Planting pattern

Once all the vital factors have been taken into consideration, it is advisable to draw up a plan of your border or bed. This can be great fun and if done properly will avoid disappointment later when a badly designed planting will show up.

The plan should be drawn to scale, preferably on grid paper. Mark out the shape of the bed or border so the positions of the groups of plants can be shown accurately. When grouping herbaceous plants, odd numbers, like three, five or seven, look better than even numbers, which tend to create straight, unnatural lines.

Irregular shaped groupings throughout the area will give the most natural effect, but while it is easy to draw squiggly lines on paper, it is more difficult to reproduce those squiggles accurately on the border or bed. Aim to produce gently flowing lines.

Mark out the lines on the surface of a smoothly raked bed with the tip of a cane or stick, then, when satisfied that it is an accurate representation of the plan, fill in the scratch marks with sand so the grand design is not washed away by the first shower of rain. The design should remain visible for quite a time, in case planting is not possible immediately.

Height
It may be obvious, but it is worth checking the ultimate height of your chosen plants. One over a metre (4 ft) taller than its neighbours will stand out embarrassingly. Height is also vital when grading the plants from tall ones at the back, to smaller at the front, as this should be gradual and neat, with a few exceptions to avoid a too artificial appearance.

Most catalogues indicate height, spread, colour and time of flowering, but treat these facts only as a guide, as plants perform differently in varying soils and climates.

Just as important as planning the herbaceous planting is making notes during the first summer, so that any necessary replanting or regrouping can be done with the experience of hindsight the next winter. These notes should include height, spread and colour.

Colour combinations
Colour photography in catalogues has improved tremendously, but colours which look good side by side in glossy magazines do not always

have the same pleasing effect in the garden. The only sure way of choosing plants successfully is to get to know them 'in the flesh'. Without knowledge plant lists are only a loose guide.

Herbaceous plants can create a riot of colour – and riots are not always pleasant to see! But harmony can be restored by using plants grown for their foliage rather than their display of floral colour. Soft, subtle shades and textures are attractive in themselves and also help set off their more flamboyant neighbours. Foliage is appreciated more now than ever before – both in the garden and in flower arranging, where form and grace play as important a role as colour. This is where hostas are most useful. Other good foliage plants are golden-leaved *Filipendula ulmaria aurea*, and the low growing silver-leaved *Veronica incana*.

A generously planted herbaceous border, bursting with colour and interest and well graded in height from front to back.

Planting

The best time for planting herbaceous beds and borders, as with most plants is during the dormant season. Using container-grown plants the season can be extended slightly further into spring. Unless a great deal of care and attention is taken, plants already in growth suddenly plunged into the border from a container may suffer a check in growth.

One common mistake is to try to cram too many plants into a given space. Give them room to grow and they will develop into healthier and more attractive plants. Too many small groups if not expertly arranged can become a hotch-potch. A simple arrangement of bold groups is more satisfactory

Herbaceous plants have a natural flowering, informal beauty.

Exploit this characteristic at the planning stage by arranging the groups so they appear to flow and mingle. This will never be achieved with rigid, square plantings.

Helpful hint

Stocking a new border or island bed in one year can be costly, because of the sheer number of plants needed to cover the area. So while the bed is still developing, fill the spaces between the young herbaceous plants with cheaper annuals, such as *Lavatera* (mallow), *Nicotiana* (tobacco plant), or *Lathyrus* (sweet pea). This will create a colourful show and still allow the herbaceous plants to build up into good-sized clumps, which can then be split to form more groups – another cost cutting measure!

Staking

Though smaller varieties of herbaceous plants have been introduced, there is still a need for some staking. If done incorrectly, or too late, the plants will not be adequately supported and an ugly mess will result.

The simplest and best method of staking is carried out when growth is young – about 15–23 cm (6–9 in) high. Twigs or very small branches are pushed into the soil at an angle around the clumps of plants that need support, forming wigwams. The top of each wigwam should be 23–30 cm (9–12 in) shorter than the anticipated height of the bottom of the flower. The plants quickly grow through the twigs, which soon become a hidden but very effective support for the soft, pliable stems. If extra support is needed, string can be tied around the wigwams. (Brown or green string is preferable to brightly coloured plastic string.)

Pests and diseases

Most herbaceous plants are pest and disease free, though some asters are prone to the fungal disease, mildew. Choose varieties that are disease resistant wherever possible, and use a preventive spray of fungicide.

Plants that are given good, healthy growing conditions tend to be far less susceptible to disease than those grown under stressful conditions. But aphids adore healthy, succulent young plants! Greenfly and blackfly also delight in sucking the juices from some herbaceous plants such as phlox, chrysanthemums and delphiniums. The only way to combat them is to use chemicals during the growing season – either 'contact' chemicals for a direct kill, or 'systemic' ones which get inside the plant to be absorbed by the aphids as they suck the juices.

Try to vary the chemicals used, as pests tend to build up resistance and immunity to one that is used regularly. Plan a system of spraying which alternates two or even three different chemicals. As manufacturers use different trade names for the same chemical, always note the *chemical* name, in small print, *not* the trade name.

Weeds

Before planting any area with herbaceous plants remove *all* perennial weeds. Borders can be ruined if they are overrun with couch grass or ground elder. Chemicals are a great help in the battle against the invaders, but it is still better to prevent them gaining a roothold than to try to eradicate them once they are established.

So start new plantings on clean soil free from perennial weeds and eradicate any signs of invasion with the newly developed chemicals designed for the purpose. A mulch will help keep down annual weeds as well as conserving moisture.

Bulbs

Along with herbaceous plants, bulbs provide splashes of seasonal colour throughout the garden. Botanically, bulbs, corms, tubers etc., are all different, but they tend to be used in much the same way, so for our purposes we can group them all together as bulbs.

Bulbs have a wide range of uses in the garden, the greenhouse and the home as flowering pot plants or cut flowers. Many flower early, long before any other group of plants stirs from winter, giving a tremendous boost to a garden otherwise devoid of floral colours.

They also have an irresistible charm. Poets have revelled among hosts of golden daffodils, the snowdrop has universal appeal, and there will always be romantic associations with a bluebell wood.

Choosing bulbs

When buying bulbs choose the best possible. Cheaper bulbs are usually smaller or of inferior quality. Always check carefully to make sure they are firm and disease free. If they have been bought in a pack, again check and discard any which show signs of disease or are going soft.

Planting

Almost all bulbs thrive best in well drained soils, and can tolerate dry conditions as the bulb itself is a food store designed to cope with drought. It is therefore foreign to most of them to grow in wet soils, where they are likely to rot.

Depth
Depth of planting is important. Most bulbs sold today are accompanied by cultural notes including optimum planting depths. A loose guide is to plant the tops of the bulbs about three times the diameter of the bulb beneath the surface – slightly deeper than this with small bulbs, slightly shallower with large ones.

Distance
It is impossible to give even a general guide to planting distances between bulbs, so it is best to follow individual cultural notes. Bulbs

should only be planted in straight lines in formal bedding schemes. Everywhere else they are best grouped to give a more pleasing, natural appearance.

They are so adaptable that even the smallest garden has room for a few, in beds or mixed borders, in patios, or in tubs or windowboxes.

Some kinds of bulbs can be very successfully naturalized in woodland gardens or lawns, provided the impatient are not allowed to cut the leaves off until several weeks after flowering! These leaves – admittedly looking forlorn and unkempt-looking – do supply the bulb with nourishment vital for the next year's flowers before they finally die off.

Some gardeners insist on tying up daffodil leaves in neat bundles. This not only looks horribly unnatural, but it does the plants no good at all. In short it is a waste of time.

Aftercare

Any bulbs which are not completely hardy should be lifted and stored dry when the foliage has died down. It pays to remove faded flower heads, unless the seeds are required, so all the energy can be used to build up the bulb for the following season. Bulbs which are being stored should always be handled with great care as if bruised the soft flesh will soon be attacked by fungal diseases.

Check them periodically after dusting the bulbs with fungicide.

Pests and diseases

Most of the diseases which affect bulbs are soil-borne. As prevention is better than cure, make sure the soil is in a suitable state before planting, use only disease-free bulbs, and if disease should appear, remove infected bulbs and burn them before it spreads.

If a patch of soil from which bulbs are lifted becomes infested with disease, do avoid planting it with bulbs in future years.

Slugs can be a particular nuisance when trying to grow bulbs in moist soils. There are many proprietary slug killers which will help reduce the problem, but where there is a heavy infestation there may be no complete solution.

Bulbs in bowls

Most bulbs grown in bowls to decorate the greenhouse or home are spring flowering and grown in bulb fibre, a cheap medium without a great deal of nutrient in it. If the bulbs are to be retained for successive years they would be better in a general John Innes compost.

Crocuses and daffodils can be planted in the bowl in which they are intended to flower, but hyacinths have an uncanny knack of flowering at different times (within a week or two) even when all treated in exactly the same way.

Growing hyacinths
To control the development of hyacinths, start them off in boxes or

Daffodils seen at their most natural, massed in grass under old trees.

deep seed trays. Cover the bottom of the box with bulb fibre. Discard any damaged or diseased bulbs, then set out the rest in the box about 5 cm (2 in) apart. Cover with bulb fibre until only the tips are showing.

The next stage is where most people go wrong. They head for the airing cupboard to force the bulbs. This will only produce straggly, weak hyacinths. Instead, take the box of bulbs outside to be 'plunged'!

Thoroughly soak the bulbs and the fibre, then cover with about 15 cm (6 in) of peat or ashes. A polythene cover is useful to protect the box from excessive rain, which could cause problems. Also surround the box with small-mesh wire-netting to stop mice digging into and eating the bulbs. Leave the bulbs like this for 10 weeks. They need all this time to develop a good root system.

After 10 weeks remove them from the plunge of peat or ashes, and bring them into a cool greenhouse, or the equivalent. Forcing them into flower will take a further six weeks, starting gently and gradually increasing the heat. If the flowers are required for a specific date e.g. Christmas, make sure the bulbs are 'plunged' 16 weeks before they are needed. Mark on the calendar when they are due to be brought inside – it is easy to loose track over 10 weeks!

Two to three weeks after they are brought inside the different size and development of the bulbs will become apparent. Group those of similar size in each bulb bowl, then the preparation will be rewarded with even-sized and developed blooms.

Specially heat treated 'prepared' bulbs are also available. These do not vary as much as unprepared bulbs, but they are more expensive.

7 ROCK GARDENS

If Mother Nature has provided a natural rocky outcrop in your garden, make the most of it – it is sheer good fortune! If she did not, it is worth cheating a bit and building one.

But be warned, it is neither quick nor easy. Photographs showing a rock garden and pool with cascading waterfalls, and streams meandering 'twixt giant boulders, do not tell of the effort involved. Cameras do not suffer from back trouble – or worse! This is not intended to put anyone off building a rock garden – it is just a word of caution.

The term 'rockery' is often used to describe a rock garden. But professional gardeners do not like the term as it conjures up a picture of barrowloads of rocks heaped incongruously upon each other, with bucketfuls of soil dumped at random among them to provide final resting places – as they often turn out to be – for the unfortunate plants.

Rock gardens are generally created not just as an interesting feature in their own right, but as an ideal environment for growing alpine plants. So whether you intend to build a rock garden in Rotherham or a scree in Scunthorpe, the guidelines are the same.

They can be situated almost anywhere in the garden, but do avoid anywhere under trees. Shade, falling leaves and water droplets will cause many problems. An open, sunny site is preferable, and the soil can be contoured to allow north, south, east or west facing areas. Complementing a water feature will create a truly natural effect, provided the pond or waterfall is not of formal design.

Having chosen the site, make absolutely sure all perennial weeds have been eradicated, or they will plague future plantings.

Raw materials

Artificial stone or concrete made to resemble natural stone can create a reasonable effect, but there is nothing like the real thing.

The type of stone chosen depends on how it is hoped the final product will look. Obviously only 'water worn' limestone will do for a water worn limestone effect. This is limestone which has been contoured by years of water washing its surfaces smooth.

But the best choice is usually the stone natural to the region in which the garden is located. It will blend in far more naturally than 'foreign' stone, and be much cheaper to transport from a local quarry!

Never buy stone without inspecting it first, otherwise the manageable rocks ordered could arrive the size of boulders. Yet they do need to be big enough to create the desired effect and match the scale of the rock garden while being firmly anchored beneath the soil. Rather like icebergs, two-thirds of rock garden stones should be beneath the surface!

Weighing up the choice (Fig. 19) the solution is to invest in a few larger 'keystones' for the focal points and then build up the rest of the rock garden with smaller rocks.

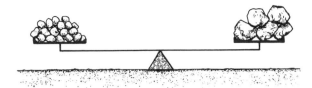

Fig. 19 Weighing up the choice. A rock garden needs a balance of large and small rocks.

Construction

Merely tipping a barrowload of rocks on site has already been dismissed as a way of constructing a rock garden. Equally unsuitable is levelling an area of soil and dotting it with rocks, irrespective of their shape, size or strata.

Strata is the term used to describe the lines in rocks made as the rocks were formed by successive layers deposited over millions of years. It is most important to take these strata lines into consideration when laying rocks. In nature they tend to run almost horizontally, and should do so in a rock garden if it is to look natural. (Fig. 20).

Geologists will know that strata do not always run horizontally, having been squeezed and folded by the movement of the earth's crust. So any geologist gardeners should feel free to create their own geological 'faults' in the rock garden. The rest of us can assume that the earth did not decide to rock and roll beneath *our* gardens.

Fig. 20 A more natural effect is created by placing the rocks with their strata on the same plane.

Moving large stones can cause a headache – and a backache! Many gardening books show large stones being moved by means of rollers across boards. However, assuming that the use of large machinery is out of the question, the easiest way is to invite some kind – and strong – friends or neighbours. Two or three are usually sufficient. Too many just get in the way.

The first stone to place should be one of the biggest and best marked, as the focal point, or 'keystone'. Then build up the others around it, complementing it and forming a natural-looking rock structure. More than one keystone can be used in a rock garden, but take care to maintain balance and harmony.

When placing the stones in the earth, dig them in and pack them firmly to stop them rocking. If they are laid back slightly rainwater will run backwards off the stone towards any plants that are grown in the crevices. The rocks also look more solid, naturally permanent features like this (Fig. 21).

Rock gardens provide an ideal environment for most alpine plants, which tend to favour well drained sites. However, some have adapted themselves to withstand extreme conditions, so the addition of scree (the result of a rock fall or avalanche) allows an even wider range of plants to be grown.

If limestone is used to construct the rock garden, it would seem logical to avoid acid loving plants, but this is not necessarily so. Pockets can be created specially for acid lovers, though they should be towards the top of the slope so that lime is not leached down into them. In nature, the droppings from sheep which graze on limestone pasture,

Never position rocks haphazardly. Follow a few simple principles, then the finished result will look natural and convincing and form a home in which the plants will thrive. Note the strata lines (*top*) and lay the rocks so they all slope back into the ground at the same angle. Arrange the rocks (*bottom left*) so that together they appear to form part of one large outcrop. (*Bottom right*) Place suitable plants, like this sempervivum (houseleek) in the crevices and pockets you have created.

change the acidity of the soil at all levels, encouraging the growth of acid-loving plants. If sheep droppings are not to hand, or considered undesirable, a handful of peat will provide an adequate substitute.

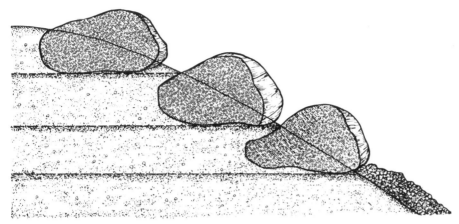

Fig. 21 Building the rock garden: cross-section diagram. When the first (lowermost) rock is placed, soil should be built up to the second horizontal line; when the second rock is placed, the soil should be built up to the third horizontal line.

Planting

When choosing plants for a rock garden, take care not to plant spreading plants, which will quickly carpet the area, too close to choice alpines. A helianthemum (rock rose, or sun rose), for example, is not a suitable neighbour for a choice gentian. Within a year the friendly helianthemum will probably have smothered the quiet little gentian with love and affection. A disconcerting situation for the gentian which prefers to keep herself to herself. Living half way up a mountain, one does not expect the neighbours to be so overwhelming.

Troughs and sinks

Having discovered that the human friends and neighbours are neither so friendly nor so neighbourly as expected, and proving somewhat reluctant to help move two-ton rocks up the garden, a full-blooded 'Mount Everest' may well be out of the question. So why not go to the other end of the scale and grow miniature gardens in sinks and troughs? The great advantage of containers like these is that various groups of plants – lime-lovers, like the *Ranunculus* (buttercups), *Primula veris* (cowslip) and potentillas, and acid-lovers such as heathers, most gentians, primulas, and saxifrages, can all be grown in the same garden but in separate containers filled with different compost.

Troughs

Stone troughs are expensive to buy, but if one happens to be lying around empty it can be put to use, and looks super when well stocked.

Most alpines prefer to grow in a free-draining, moisture-retentive medium. 'Impossible!', goes up the cry. Not necessarily. Ample grit and sand will provide free drainage, while the peat content will hold moisture.

Unless the intention is to grow specialist plants, there is no need to worry too much about the compost used. If it is based on John Innes

No. I compost (without lime for ericaceous types) and you add more peat and grit to create the conditions described above, it should do good service.

Sinks
Failing a stone trough, perhaps you possess an old glazed porcelain sink, which had long been under the threat of the sledge hammer. A stay of execution and an application of 'gunge' will transform it into a good imitation of a stone trough!

'Gunge' is a *non*-technical term, which here means a mixture of sand, cement, peat and water. The technical name is 'hypertufa', which, when dried and weathered on a sink will give it a reasonably natural appearance. However, a word of warning! The mixture will not stick straight on the shiny surface of a sink. In the old days it was necessary to chip off the glazed enamel with hammer and chisel, but nowadays there are several popular bonding agents (such as Polybond or Unibond) which will stick to the sink and then allow the 'gunge' to stick to them.

The sand, cement, peat mix can be an equal parts mixture, though slightly more peat can be added for a better finish. If a small amount of riddled peat is dusted or blown on to the sticky surface of the mix this will help it to become weathered looking more quickly.

Another way of speeding up the weathering process is to encourage mosses and lichens to grow on the surface. This needs a strong stomach, as it involves painting the surface with a thick, sticky mixture of cow dung and milk!

As with all plant containers there is the danger of drying out in summer. Take great care to prevent this happening as their restricted root run will mean that the plants have no scope to delve further into the earth to avoid drought.

Other homes for alpines
Alpines do not have to have a special home created for them in a rock garden or trough. They can be grown equally successfully among paving stones or in walls.

Stone retaining walls are often needed somewhere in the garden, if there is a sunken drive or a raised flower bed, and can be greatly enhanced by growing alpines in or over them. But before planting, take careful note of the wall's aspect, which will recreate the conditions on a particular side of the mountain where the alpines grow. Then choose the most suitable plants for each site.

If they can be planted while the wall is being built, so much the better. It is much easier to plant in a niche, then place the next stone over it, than trying to push delicate roots into small crevices in an existing wall.

When building a retaining wall start with the largest stones at the bottom to stabilize the whole structure. If it can be built on an angle (slightly laid back) this will give added strength.

Alpines really are little gems in the garden, and there should be at least one spot where they can be grown.

WATER FEATURES

8

Water is fun. For centuries it has provided a source of fascination for Man – and Woman: to stare into and watch how it twists and contorts the shapes of objects beneath its surface; to wonder at the different forms of life that develop in it; to bathe in, and be enchanted by the sound of a babbling brook or raging waterfall.

As a result, water features have always enjoyed a place in large gardens, sometimes simply as an expanse of open lake, elsewhere as magnificent cascades or fountains. Such features were regarded as signs of opulence and good taste. But they are expensive to create.

Today, water features can be constructed more cheaply on a comparatively small scale with modern materials. Done carefully and tastefully, a pool can transform a previously dull garden into a vibrant, magical place which will give endless hours of pleasure to all. But haphazard construction can create a cheap and nasty eyesore.

Size and shape

The dimensions of a pool will be determined by the style and size of the garden. If the garden is laid out in a formal style with rectangular borders and straight lines a formal shaped pool is probably the only choice. A more natural layout allows a much wider choice of shapes.

There are many pre-formed pools on sale. Some have a natural-looking shape. Others look more like a sausage after a bad accident!

When choosing the size and shape of a pool remember that the larger the pool the easier it is to maintain the correct balance of nature. Also remember that a pool will need an edging of stone or grass, and that jagged edges will be difficult to soften in stone, and awkward to mow if grassed.

When Mother Nature created streams, lakes, pools and waterfalls she did a perfectly satisfactory job without having to employ obvious lumps of cement to bind stones together, or vivid blue polythene liners which peep through every gap. So try to copy some of the examples she designed and you will not go too far astray!

Site

Where pools are given an open, sunny site they will generally do well. But a shady, overcast site will tend to produce algae at a rapid rate. Overhanging trees can be a major problem too. The weeping branches of certain trees and shrubs may look picturesque, but the leaves they shed will rot and turn any water below into a foul-smelling morass.

Construction

There are many ways of creating a garden pool. Some are more effective than others, some are easier.

Creating a pool with a pre-formed rigid plastic liner. Excavate carefully to take the liner exactly, then set it in place. Check that it is level, so that when filled the surface of the water lies parallel with the top of the pool.

Concrete

New concrete pools need to be filled and left for a while to allow any harmful salts to dissolve out. The water then needs to be properly drained before refilling and stocking the pool with plants and fish.

Concrete is still used for large ponds, but the vast amount of work this involves and the problems of cracking and leaking mean that other materials are more suitable for small garden pools.

Polythene

Heavy duty polythene sheets are relatively cheap, but only last a couple of years before deteriorating and starting to leak.

PVC

Nylon and Butyl are now frequently used as pool liners. They are more expensive, but are longer lasting.

When using a pool liner, remember that the more complicated the shape, the more waste there will be. When calculating the amount of liner required a useful guide is:

Length of liner = length of pool + *twice* maximum depth of pool
Width of liner = width of pool + *twice* maximum depth

Preformed pools

These have revolutionized water gardening. Though initially expensive, they often have a guaranteed life of ten years. All you need do is select the size and shape to suit your garden and dig the appropriate hole!

Whether using a preformed pool or building your own, make allowance for a shelf or ledge round the edge of the pool for growing marginal plants (Fig. 22). Similar conditions can be provided in pools without a ledge, by stacking stones to the desired height, and planting on top of those.

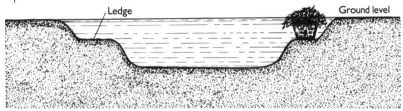

Ledge · Ground level

Fig. 22 Cross-section of a pool. Shelves or ledges enable marginal plants to be grown.

Whichever type of pool you choose, take great care to ensure that sharp stones do not puncture it. Sand or sieved soil can be used to cushion anything that threatens damage.

Cascades and waterfalls

Like pools, cascades and waterfalls are also available in the materials described above. Again, edges should be disguised or hidden, or the completed feature will look false and unpleasant. Always try to re-create what nature has achieved – the results will be far more pleasing (Fig. 23).

The best water features are constructed from natural stone, of course (see Chapter 7).

Fig. 23 Disguise any artificial edges of a water cascade to create a more natural effect.

Pumps

When recirculating water with a pump, take expert advice as to the size required. Submersible pumps are easy to install. Place the pump in the water, fit a hose pipe and direct it into the inlet. If the inlet is made to look like a natural spring, so much the better (Fig. 24).

All electrical connections should be waterproof. If unsure, take no chances but consult a qualified electrician.

Fig. 24 Using a submersible pump and running the hosepipe underground can create the same effect as a natural spring.

Most pumps are sold with the performance indicated in gallons per hour (gph). A useful guide is that a flow of 300 gph will produce a thin sheet of water over a width of 15 cm (6 in). But the output of a pump depends partly on the height to which water has to be raised. Always check the manufacturer's performance charts.

Additional equipment

Fountain kits – various patterns are available.

Heaters – used in winter to prevent the surface freezing over completely.

Lighting – underwater lighting can greatly enhance the pool. If the water feature is natural in appearance only use the most subtle lighting effect.

However, exotic fountains and colourful lighting arrangements can be extremely attractive on large, formal pools.

Planting

Planting direct into water is not as easy or straightforward as planting into soil. Unless great care is taken the result could be a very muddy pool. The cleanest and most efficient way is to use specially designed plastic planting baskets, available in a variety of sizes (Fig. 25).

Line the inside of the basket with hessian to stop the soil washing away. Secure the plants firmly in fairly heavy soil with a high clay content, that has not recently been treated with fertilizer.

A layer of pea gravel on top of the soil will reduce disturbance when it is placed in the water – and also stop fish playing in the mud later!

Fig. 25 A layer of pea gravel spread over the compost in the planting basket helps to keep the pond clean and stops it becoming a mud bath.

Unlike land plants, water plants are best planted during their growing season – generally between April and September.

Water plants fall into several categories.

Marginals

These thrive in conditions ranging from wet soil to shallow water up to 15 cm (6 in) deep. Several members of the iris family belong here, including the variegated *Iris laevigata variegata* with its soft, blue flowers. Another good marginal plant is *Caltha palustris* (marsh marigold or kingcup) of which there are both yellow and white forms.

Oxygenating plants

These grow beneath the surface, producing the oxygen so essential for fish, and are generally known as pondweeds.

They are bought in bunches of unrooted cuttings, often fastened together with a weight, and simply dropped into the water and left to mature.

Surface-flowering aquatics

These, including water lilies, root into soil well below the surface of the water. They often have large leaves, so are useful for providing shade for fish.

Free-floating aquatics

This group of plants includes some that like to wander. In the cold of winter *Stratiotes aloides* (water soldier) submerges into the depths of the pool, then floats up to the surface again in the summer to bask and flower. Others in this group are happy to remain on the surface all year round.

In order to create a balanced plant life in pools, many specialist nurseries offer 'collections' of plants designed to suit the needs of a particular size of pool.

Water snails

While water plants will help to keep the pool alive and healthy, the addition of those slimy little molluscs, water snails, will do sterling work in keeping it clean.

Fish

Although the pool itself adds an extra dimension to the garden it is not really complete until it contains at least a goldfish or two. But fish, like gardeners, are extremely sensitive creatures and should be treated as such. After the pool has been planted, at least a couple of weeks should elapse before stocking with fish.

When deciding how many fish to introduce, a guideline is that 30 sq cm (I sq ft) of pool is capable of supporting a fish 5 cm (2 in) in length. Using this guide it is easy to work out the total area of pond and how many 'big 'uns' and 'little 'uns' it can accommodate.

The names of fish are almost as daunting as the names of plants, but going to a specialist will help you choose between shibunkins, orfe, koi carp and many others.

When introducing fish to the pool keep them in a polythene bag on the water surface for at least half an hour so the temperature of the water around them can adjust to that of the pool — otherwise the shock of release could be too much for them.

Pests and diseases

Like every other living organism, fish can be affected by pests and diseases. Next door's cat will require a deterrent to fit the individual, or your own inclination! Predatory herons, however, can be deterred by cotton threads stretched across the pool.

If fish are found floating or gasping at the surface of the water, this does not indicate a previous evening of over-indulgence! It is more likely to mean they are short of oxygen, probably because there are too many fish in too small a pool.

Whenever fish are ailing and lethargic they should be removed and kept in a separate container where they can be treated, and will not contaminate the other inhabitants of the pool.

I (Alan Mason) remember having one goldfish which used to *pretend* to be ill every three weeks because my father used to put it in a goldfish bowl and add a few drops of whisky to the water. I don't know of any good reason why this should revive the fish, but it certainly seemed to work. It is not something I would recommend, and am sure you can find a better use for the whisky!

Take great care when using chemicals and fertilizers in a garden containing a pond, as they can easily contaminate the water.

Having taken such great care designing, planting and stocking your pool, sit back at a safe distance and enjoy it!

The completed surroundings of the pool (p.66) its edges masked with paving. The background is dominated by rockwork, a golden conifer and a dainty Japanese maple.

9

THE GREENHOUSE OR CONSERVATORY

A heated greenhouse or conservatory does not offer a cheap form of gardening, but it can certainly provide one of the most rewarding and enjoyable hobbies. Imagine, on a cold, frosty morning, when even the birds are coughing, the pleasure of a hot, humid atmosphere with tropical flowers and vegetables thriving in a plants' paradise. The feeling of well-being, knowing that gardening can continue right through the year, is indeed something to cherish – at least until the heating bill arrives!

But there are no rules stating that greenhouses *have* to be heated. In fact many plants can be grown without the luxury of extra heat.

Conservatories were popular in Victorian times. The term was then used to describe elaborate plant houses used to display a vast array of foliage and flowering plants. The plants were usually grown in ordinary greenhouses elsewhere.

Today's conservatory is generally a lean-to structure built on the home, and is used for growing as well as displaying plants. It can also perform the extra duty of being a garden room. Some elegant designs are available including some that are double glazed.

The conservatory used as an extra room is becoming increasingly popular, sometimes to the exclusion of all but a few choice specimen plants. The glazed structure can therefore be a versatile addition to any garden and should be chosen carefully.

Choosing a greenhouse or conservatory

It is not always easy to visualize what you might require of it in two or three years' time, but if a degree of flexibility can be achieved in the choice of structure, so much the better. Some glasshouses can have extra sections added later. Other, larger ones, can have partitions installed so that only certain sections need be heated. Cheap bargains, however, can turn out to be costly mistakes.

Materials
Generally greenhouses and conservatories are made of wood or aluminium. Wooden structures can be more elaborate in design, and are warmer than metal, which cuts fuel bills. The glazing bars need to be more substantial though, than their metal counterparts, which reduces the amount of light entering. This is not of paramount importance in summer, but can be vital in winter.

Some structures are built with glass to the floor, others with wooden or brick sides. The former lose heat more quickly than the latter but are far more suitable for crops grown at ground level, such as lettuces. If pot plants are to be grown on benches, the solid sided design is preferable. Bear in mind that wooden structures need routine maintenance such as painting, whereas aluminium houses only need the glass cleaning.

When choosing a greenhouse or conservatory check the glazing system. If the glass breaks for any reason (the neighbouring children's football) replacing fancy shaped pieces in the roof may be not only difficult, but also extremely dangerous. And some glazing systems leave gaps through which expensive heat rapidly sails away.

Access

In larger greenhouses or conservatories it helps if you can use a wheelbarrow inside when clearing out. So access is important and a large wide door is essential.

Ventilation

Do not be tempted to save a few pounds by skimping on the number of ventilators. Ample ventilation in summer is vital to the growth of healthy plants, as well as to the comfort of the perspiring human form if it is a garden room. Most professional greenhouses have a ventilated area equivalent to about a third of the total floor space.

Kits are available to open and close ventilators when the desired temperature has been reached. These are particularly useful when you cannot keep dashing out to open them manually, and during holidays.

Siting the glasshouse

While siting the structure is often determined by other local factors, aim to get maximum light into it. Protection from wind, by natural or specially created windbreaks, is also essential to cut down the heating costs.

Heating

Before installing any form of heating, give careful thought to the types of plants you want to grow, as this will determine the temperature requirement.

For any form of heating to be efficient, it should be very strictly controlled. Heat that is provided unnecessarily is sheer waste. Accurate thermostats quickly pay for their initial cost. It is not always realized that for every 2.8°C (5°F) the temperature is raised, the cost virtually increases by 100 per cent.

Glasshouses that can be plumbed in to the domestic central heating system can be heated most efficiently. Where this is not possible the alternatives must be considered carefully.

Electricity

Heating with electricity can be expensive, but it is one of the most accurately controlled, trouble free and automated methods of heating available to the amateur. But beware! Loose or exposed wiring in a humid greenhouse (particularly a metal one) can really make things go with a bang. Electricity supplies installed by amateur Mr Fixits can prove hazardous, if not lethal! If you are not competent to install electricity safely, make sure it is done by someone who is.

Electric heating can be provided by tubular heaters, fan heaters or heating cables.

Tubular heaters are usually fastened to the sides of the greenhouse. They have to be tough and waterproof and are generally made of aluminium. Depending on how much heat is required, they can be used singly or in tiers. As with all heating installations, make sure you use an accurate thermostat.

Fan heaters operate by blowing air over heating elements and distributing the warm air around the glasshouse. This air movement can be extremely beneficial in deterring fungal disease (a major winter problem under glass). But warm air that constantly batters plant foliage can be harmful, so try to position the fan to avoid this.

Alternatively, particularly in a large greenhouse, the heat can be distributed evenly throughout the length of the house through polythene tubes or perforated ducts, making sure the polythene is not in danger of melting near the fan and becoming a hazard.

Ducting bought without holes should be perforated with smaller holes near the fan and larger ones further away so that the heat is spread evenly. Holes made at the bottom of the ducting direct heat towards the plants (Fig. 26).

Fig. 26 Polythene ducting is a cheap and effective method of transporting heat to where it is required.

Heating for plants growing on benches can be sited above them and directed downwards. The ducting can be supported by a wire threaded through it. The end furthest from the fan needs to be blocked by simply tying it.

The fan in many fan heaters works continuously, while the heating elements are operated by a thermostat. However, some models turn off both the heater and the fan when the right temperature is reached, and are cheaper to run than the first type.

Heating cables

These can be used to raise the temperature of benches, propagation beds and even the air temperature of enclosed frames (Fig. 27). Cables can also provide both soil and air space heating, or each separately depending on whether warm soil is required for propagation, or air warming for overwintering slightly tender plants in a frame.

Paraffin heaters

The cheapest heater to install is probably the paraffin burner. Despite

A greenhouse with solid timber or brick sides is well suited for growing pot plants on staging. There is plenty of light and the sides help to retain a little extra warmth.

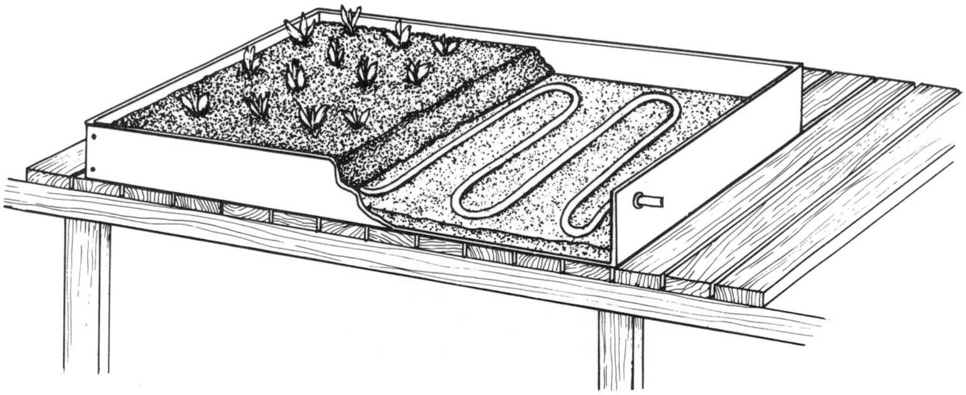

Fig. 27 Soil warming cables are a cost effective method of heating a propagating frame. (When in use, the cable is, of course, connected to a suitable electrical outlet.)

the increase in the price of paraffin they are still relatively inexpensive to run, but they do require regular maintenance, otherwise problems will arise due to inefficient burning.

Use only high grade fuel to avoid trouble from excess fumes. The wick must be regularly trimmed and adjusted and the fuel tank topped up regularly. These heaters are not thermostatically controlled. Oil burners are quite adequate if only basic frost protection is required, but not if one hankers after a tropical paradise.

Gas
Bottled gas heaters offer a fairly controllable form of heating. Problems arise if the cylinders empty during the middle of a frosty night. However, if precautions are taken to prevent this happening or where convenient domestic gas from the mains can be used to supply a suitable heater, gas can be a useful method of heating.

Solid fuel
Solid fuel heating is not normally used in small greenhouses, but it is still available for larger structures. With this system a burner or stove can provide heat directly when sited in the greenhouse (provided a flue chimney is used). More often the boiler heats water, which warms the greenhouse with a circuit of pipes. If this system appeals to you, it is vital to get expert advice on the size of boiler and pipework, as installation costs are high. Unless the system is designed efficiently and effectively money can be quickly wasted.

Insulation

Some conservatories are made with double glazing, an extra initial cost that must be considered a long-term investment. Many cheap constructions are too draughty, and should be avoided at all costs, though heat loss can be reduced by proper insulation.

Several materials are now available today which allow light to be transmitted, but keep the heat inside the glasshouse. They can reduce the heating bill by as much as 30 per cent.

Polythene 'bubble' material, similar to that used for packaging delicate goods, and plastic interlacing (which has the same effect as a string vest) can be fastened to the walls and roof. Commercial growers also reduce the size of the heated area on winter nights by pulling on a 'thermal screen' just over the top of the plants, which saves heating the roof space (Fig. 28).

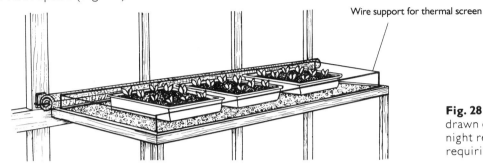

Wire support for thermal screen

Fig. 28 A thermal screen drawn over the plants at night reduces the area requiring heat.

Shading

In summer, besides ventilating the greenhouse to lower the temperature, it is also shaded. This stops the sun scorching delicate foliage too. Shading can be provided in the form of netting rolled over the top of the plants or suspended in the air, or by simply painting the glass with a shading paint.

Watering

Watering plants under glass is as important as temperature control. Irrigation systems are on sale, but are not popular with amateurs. Two methods that can be used successfully are perforated hosepipes and capillary matting. A perforated hosepipe can be used to water beds of lettuces or tomatoes, for example. The supply is simply turned on and left until sufficient water has been introduced (Fig. 29).

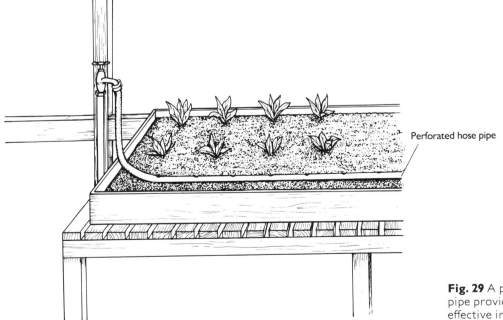

Perforated hose pipe

Fig. 29 A perforated hose pipe provides uniform and effective irrigation.

77

Capillary matting

This is a moisture-retentive 'carpet' used on greenhouse benches on which pot plants stand taking up the amount of water they need. This system is only suitable for the summer as it tends to hold too much moisture in winter.

Plastic plant pots are best for this system as they have thin bottoms and the compost can more easily come into contact with the matting. If clay pots are used, put a wick through the bottom of the pot to ensure contact between matting and compost.

Capillary matting needs a water supply from a hosepipe, manual watering, or from a perforated hosepipe (Fig. 30).

Liquid feeding can be applied by either method.

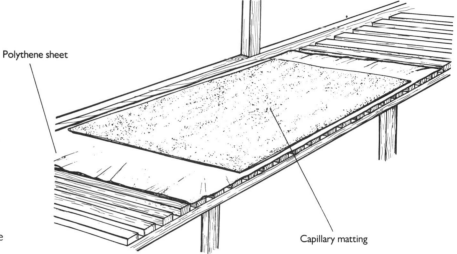

Polythene sheet

Capillary matting

Fig. 30 A polythene sheet beneath capillary matting prevents valuable moisture being lost.

Humidity

The greenhouse atmosphere needs to be kept humid in summer for most plants. This can be achieved by spraying the paths and walls with water while there is enough heat left in the day for evaporation.

In winter there is a great tendency to overwater pot plants. They are far better left rather on the dry side than becoming too moist.

Plants for the greenhouse or conservatory

The protection afforded by a cold greenhouse is sufficient even in the North to grow the most succulent peaches and glorious grapes, particularly if the structure is facing south so it receives maximum ripening sunshine. Salad crops, lettuces, tomatoes and cucumbers also thrive in a cold glasshouse. Plants that are not fully hardy can also be grown, which extends the range of the collection.

Bulbs are a popular choice for early colour, and are often grown among alpine plants. Alpines grown under glass are not there for the heat it provides as they are totally hardy, but for the protection it gives from the rain.

If the glasshouse is heated the range of possible plants multiplies several times over. When buying plants, instructive labels or advice from the grower are invaluable when determining temperature and water requirements. However, most plants tend to be hardier than once imagined, so it pays to experiment a little. Just because the label says 15°C (60°F) it does not mean it might not be equally successful at 10°C (50°F), and this will make a considerable difference to your heating bill.

Summer colour in a temperate conservatory. The colourful plants in the foreground are streptocarpus, backed by *Whitfieldia elongata* (white blooms) and ivy (*Hedera Lelix* 'Goldheart').

Pests and diseases

The gentle, easy atmosphere of the glasshouse can be a holiday camp for friends and relations of a vast array of pests and diseases. For this reason hygiene is tremendously important under glass. If meticulous standards of cleanliness are adopted for the glass, walls and paths, the growing conditions for the plants will be greatly enhanced.

When leaves start to yellow with age, or are damaged in any other way, they should be removed cleanly and disposed of (*not* under the bench to decay).

Most pests and diseases can be overcome by pesticides in the form of sprays or smokes. Particular care must be taken when growing a mixed collection of plants that the chemicals used will not damage any of the plants. Early application – not at 5.30 a.m.! – before the pest or disease becomes established is obviously best. It may be possible to spot-treat individual outbreaks.

Hygiene is just as important for composts and containers. Use sterilized compost to avoid starting off with pots full of weeds, pests and diseases. Containers should always be clean and if possible sterilized for the same reason.

Composts

In the heyday of the large private gardens a great deal of mystery surrounded the composts used. The head gardener had his own magical, closely guarded recipes for individual plants. The advent of the John Innes range of composts, however, changed all this by providing a growing medium in which all but the most faddy plants would thrive.

John Innes composts are based on sterilized loam mixed with peat and sand.

The recipe for John Innes No. I is:

    7 parts partially sterilized loam
    3 parts peat   (All parts by bulk)
    2 parts sand
    To every 35 l (8 gallons) of the above mixture add 20 g ($\frac{3}{4}$ oz) ground limestone and 120 g (4 oz) of fertilizer in the following proportions:
    2 parts hoof and horn
    2 parts superphosphate of lime
    I part sulphate of potash

The advantage of a loam-based compost is that the loam acts as a buffer during base exchange, which simply means there are less likely to be feeding problems in such a compost. Plants to be grown and kept for longer than one growing season usually do better in John Innes composts.

As loam of good quality has become more difficult to obtain, the range of loamless composts has increased. These are good, but if allowed to dry out they are usually extremely difficult to re-wet, so never let them get bone dry. What's more, dry compost is very light, so the plant becomes top heavy and is more likely to blow over if it is in a plastic plant pot.

PROPAGATION

10

Propagation is one of the most exciting aspects of gardening. To be able to take some part of a plant and produce a whole new plant gives even the experienced gardener a special thrill and sense of achievement. Some propagation can be carried out without a greenhouse, but having one makes it much easier.

Nature's most prolific way of propagation is by seeds. Large numbers can be produced, though with some trees and shrubs this can take a very long time. Some cultivated plants do not come true from seed. That is, the offspring from the seeds are different from the parent plants because two different species have interbred. Other methods of propagation then have to be used, such as cuttings, layering or division.

Seed sowing

Vast numbers of seeds of different species from all over the world can be grown, but the basics of seed sowing remain the same.

Sowing under glass in trays or pans

The container used should be clean and preferably sterilized. The basic seed tray is ideal for the vast majority of seeds, with a suitable depth of compost, sufficient to support the seedlings until they are ready to be pricked out.

For certain seeds the extra depth of a pan (a fat little plant pot) will be needed, as for example certain slow germinating shrubs which have large seeds.

Suitable compost, whether John Innes or loamless, should be finely riddled. A loamless compost which contains sand as well as peat is advantageous as it breaks up easily when the delicate seedlings are pricked out, so there is the least possible damage to their roots. Most seeds appreciate a light covering of finely riddled compost or sand during germination.

An extra cover, in the form of a sheet of paper helps to keep the seed tray dark (some seeds need darkness to germinate successfully) and will also provide a little extra warmth.

The first signs of those tiny, living seedlings pushing relentlessly through the compost gives every gardener sense of excitement, no matter how old or experienced. The success of bringing life to those dust particles (which is what a lot of seeds look like) becomes no less thrilling with the years.

After germination comes the time for pricking out! Experience tells precisely when is the best time, but the general rule is to prick out early. The root systems of larger seedlings are more easily damaged, and growth can suffer a check.

It is best to keep young plants growing evenly, as a check to growth, coupled with any damage, could well encourage diseases to attack.

Make some new plants the easy way from leaf cuttings. *Top left:* Preparing a streptocarpus leaf.

Begonia rex cuttings. *Top right:* Nicking the veins.

Always hold seedlings by their seed leaves (cotyledons) to avoid damaging their stems.

Bedding plants are usually pricked out into trays, but individual plants are put straight into small pots. Don't be tempted to put a delicate seedling into a large pot. Tiny roots don't take kindly to mass of cold, wet compost, and rather than go exploring are more likely to shrivel up and die.

Bottom left: Weighting down on compost to root. *Bottom right:* New plants developing.

Cuttings

There are many different ways of taking cuttings, using every part of the plant. Some plants propagate best from leaf or stem cuttings, others from root cuttings.

The most popular form of cutting is the stem or tip cutting. This is where the top 8–10 cm (3–4 in) of a non-flowering shoot is taken with a clean cut usually just below a leaf joint or node. Internodal cuttings can be taken from such plants as fuchsias, but nodal cuttings are generally preferred. Non-flowering shoots are used because these put all their effort into producing roots and growing into healthy new plants,

rather than trying to produce flowers. Cuttings with flower buds intact will try to bloom and set seed using up valuable energy.

Left: Taking a stem cutting with four leaf joints from a geranium. *Right:* Preparing the cutting by removing the lower leaves and cutting across just beneath a leaf joint.

Side shoots can be taken and gently torn away from the main plant. This gives a cutting with a 'heel' from which roots develop prolifically.

Cuttings taken from new growth early in the season are known as softwood cuttings. These root quickly but because of their soft, sappy nature can also die much more easily in unfavourable conditions.

Hardwood cuttings are much hardier and though they take longer to root do not require much specialist attention.

In general cuttings like cool tops and warm bottoms. It will help if the top (leafy) growth of the cutting can be kept moist. Take care with silver or grey-leaved plants though, as they tend to be hairy and hold moisture, which can set up rotting. An enclosed frame or propagating case holds moisture and creates the required conditions (Fig. 31).

Cuttings root well in open, well drained, but moisture-retentive mediums. A 50/50 mix of peat and grit or sand or peat and Perlite or Vermiculite is suitable to line the floor of the propagating frame or container in which the cuttings are rooted. When containers are used, the floor of the case should be covered with sand, especially when heating cables are used as the heat spreads uniformly through sand.

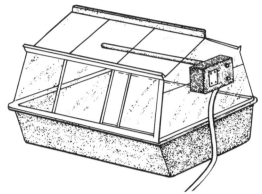

Fig. 31 An electrical propagator provides the optimum conditions for growing plants and seeds.

Great care should be taken to prevent the cuttings from drying out. Spraying the leaves with a syringe or watering can with a fine rose (the perforated end of the watering can) can be sufficient, as the moisture is retained by the lid of the case.

Provide the case frame with as much light as possible. Shading can easily be given if necessary.

A propagating frame can be compared to the maternity ward of a busy hospital, turning out babies by the score, so great care has to be taken to combat disease. Hygienic conditions must be rigorously maintained. If any leaves turn yellow, remove them before decay sets in.

Initially, the new cuttings desperately need the frame closed to ensure high humidity. But once they begin to form roots, they take on a degree of independence as they start to take up the moisture they need. This is a gradual process, so weaning them to cope with harder conditions must also be gradual.

Once the cuttings are settled in comfortably, and standing up proudly, a little air can be given by lifting the lid for short periods. As rooting progresses the lid can be lifted higher and for longer until eventually it can be removed altogether.

Hardwood cuttings are taken at the end of the growing season when the wood has ripened. These cuttings, which have lost all their leaves, do not dry out quickly like softwood cuttings. This is a very reliable method for plants such as forsythia, willows, gooseberries and blackcurrants.

Fig. 32 Hardwood cuttings are planted direct into a prepared trench making sure they are not upside down! A flat cut at the base and a sloping cut at the tip eliminates confusion.

84

The ideal hardwood cutting is pencil thick and pencil length (20–25 cm, 8–10 in). Cut the base just beneath a bud, the top just above bud. The prepared cuttings can be lined out in trenches with a little gritty sand in the bottom. These cuttings are usually taken between October and December, though it can be done later. Winter frosts may lift the cuttings, so check them periodically and firm them in again when necessary.

If several cuttings are taken of shrubs with small buds, making a sloping cut at one end and a straight cut at the other will help to distinguish the top of the cutting from the bottom. (Fig. 32). The cuttings need to be left for about a year to root well before they are lifted and planted out in the garden.

Layering

A successful method of propagation, but again it requires at least a full season. Layering often ensures success with some rhododendrons and other plants which are difficult to propagate from cuttings.

When layering, look for a branch which can be bent to the ground. It needs to be nicked at the point where it reaches the soil by making a cut about 2.5–4 cm (1–1½ in) along the length of the shoot (Fig. 33). This cut should then be held open with a sliver of wood or a tiny stone to stop both sides healing together.

Improve the soil where the layer is in contact with the ground by forking in peat and grit or sand. Then hold the cut part of the stem down in the compost, cover it with the mixture and peg the branch down or hold it in place with a large stone. Apart from watering to prevent it drying out, leave the cutting alone to develop roots. This it should do within 12 months, after which the cutting can be severed from its parent.

The cutting can be severed in the summer, but it is usually better to leave roots and shoots undisturbed until the following autumn. Plants produced in this way can be staked while being layered so their initial growth is not unbalanced (Fig. 34).

There are many other ways of propagating plants, but these methods are by way of a gentle introduction to one of gardening's most fascinating aspects.

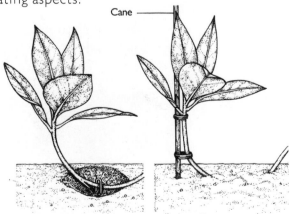

Cane

Fig. 33 (Far left) Layering is used on plants which are difficult to propagate by other methods. **Fig. 34** (Left) The layered plant is staked to prevent unbalanced growth.

11 FRUIT AND VEGETABLES

What is the purpose of a garden? Some people consider it should be purely ornamental. A sumptuous herbaceous border, brightly coloured annuals and exotic shrubs. They would think growing vegetables a waste of time as produce can be bought cheaply and more enjoyment can be gained from the visual feast of ornamental plants.

To others their garden is a fruit and vegetable plot. It may be a part of the whole garden area kept specifically as the productive area, or it can be a completely separate garden or allotment. These gardeners believe that home grown produce tastes much better than mass-produced fruit and vegetables. It is fresher and they have had total control over any chemical sprays used.

Thankfully, there is a third group of gardeners who fully appreciate both schools of thought, and make room on their plot for a flower garden and an area for growing food.

Vegetables

To the avid vegetable grower his plot is sacred ground, and planning and planting it a highly organized procedure. A vegetable plot is traditionally divided into three distinct areas. These may only be in the gardener's mind but a diagram is often useful. The reason for the division of the plot is all to do with the rotation of crops which we first heard about in agricultural history lessons at school. The theory behind it is to avoid planting the same crop in the same area of soil each year, so that diseases do not get a chance to build up.

The rotation of crops is vital in agriculture, but within the confines of an average garden most pests and diseases could, in fact, walk, fly, or even hitch a lift to the neighbouring plot to do their evil deeds. Yet it *is* still worth practising in the garden as it does offer some disease control, makes weed control easier, and gives some semblance of order to the application of manure. Some crops like liberal dressings, others only a light application.

The normal rotation system is carried out over a three year period (Fig. 35). The rotational guide shows that lime is applied every three years. Lime corrects over-acidity, bringing the pH to neutral. The only way to determine a soil's lime requirement is to take a soil pH (acidity/alkalinity) test. Using lime can also help reduce the effects of clubroot in brassicas.

Digging
Work in the vegetable garden does not start in spring with seed sowing, but back in the autumn with some stout exercise – digging (Fig. 36). To dig over a plot successfully, start by taking out a trench at point A and dumping the soil at point B, so there is soil available to fill in the final trench. Digging like this leaves the garden exposed to winter frosts, which break down the large clods of earth.

A pyramid of strawberries grown in 18 cm, 20 cm and 25 cm (7 in, 8 in and 10 in) pots one on top of another – fine for a tasty early crop in a small space.

Seed sowing

In spring, as the soil warms up, preparations for seed sowing begin. Rake the soil level and break down any large lumps that remain. Where soils are difficult to work, it may be necessary to fork the area lightly before raking. Treading the soil gently to firm it and a final raking should produce the tilth required for a seedbed – fine crumbly surface soil in which seeds will readily germinate.

The soil should not be over wet at this stage, or it could become over-compacted, making it extremely difficult to break down into the small crumbs required. In fact, if the soil is too wet for treading and

87

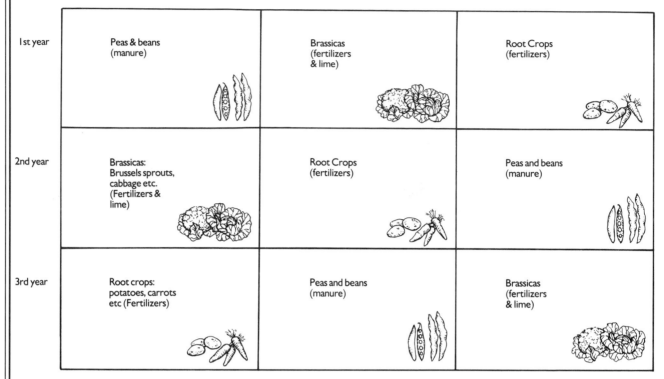

1st year	Peas & beans (manure)	Brassicas (fertilizers & lime)	Root Crops (fertilizers)
2nd year	Brassicas: Brussels sprouts, cabbage etc. (Fertilizers & lime)	Root Crops (fertilizers)	Peas and beans (manure)
3rd year	Root crops: potatoes, carrots etc (Fertilizers)	Peas and beans (manure)	Brassicas (fertilizers & lime)

Fig. 35 Rotation of crops over a three-year period.

raking, keep off it. If on the other hand the soil is particularly dry, water it before sowing seeds.

Seed merchants usually provide precise cultural details on their seed packets – and not just for the benefit of the gardener. If for any reason the seeds fail, it is easy to blame the seedsman and his seeds and go to a rival the following year. The cultural details are his protection. They describe the optimum conditions in which his seeds should be sown, and if followed carefully there should be few problems.

The preparation of a seedbed is the same for most vegetable seeds. Only the sowing depth and width of drill vary. (A drill is the name given to the shallow trench in which the seeds are sown.)

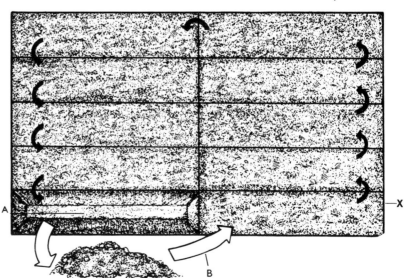

Fig. 36 Digging a plot. First divide the plot in half. Then dig trench 'A'. Retain soil to fill in final trench 'X'. Fill in trench 'A' with soil removed from 'B'. Continue digging and filling. (Arrows show direction of soil).

Having trodden and raked the soil, the seed drill is made with a hoe or the edge of a rake (Fig. 37). A taut garden line is essential, as a guide to ensure the vegetables do not emerge in untidy, wavy rows.

Fig. 37 Making a seed drill by means of taut garden line and hoe.

The most popular method of sowing seeds is to scatter them gently between finger and thumb. But some gardeners just form a 'V' in the seed packet and sow them direct.

Immediately after sowing, cover the seeds with the finely raked soil. Gently and carefully rake the soil back over the drill, making sure the seeds are not scattered in many directions. Where larger seeds have been buried more deeply, it is more effective to adopt the 'soft shoe shuffle' technique – with heels together and toes apart, shuffle forward, pushing the soil back into the trench, rather like a snow plough in reverse.

Having sown the seeds and covered them, make sure that the ends of the rows are marked and clearly labelled. Those vegetables that need thinning out should be thinned progressively rather than in one major operation. Then if some of them die, others can be thinned to fill the gaps.

On heavy soil that easily over-compacts it is a good idea to work from a plank whenever possible as this spreads one's weight over a larger area.

Stagger the sowing dates of vegetables like radishes and lettuces through the season to avoid a glut, though these days most surplus vegetables can be frozen.

Planting potatoes

Potatoes may seem to need a completely different method of growing from other vegetables, but there are similarities. The seed drill becomes a definite 'trench' of 13–15 cm (5–6 in) deep and the 'seeds' are covered just like other seeds. However, as the shoots emerge and grow, they should be 'earthed up' – the soil is drawn up over the stems and tubers to keep them completely covered. If light reaches the potato tubers it will turn them green and make them inedible.

Planting distances
This has been the subect of much research in recent years. The results show, as one might expect, that closer planting produces smaller vegetables than wider spacing, but at the same time the yield per given area is often greater.

The following is merely a guide to show the average planting distances between the various vegetables:

Cabbages	35–45 cm (14–18 in) apart (in and between rows)
Cauliflowers	45–60 cm (18–24 in) apart (in and between rows)
Brussels Sprouts	60 cm (2 ft) apart (in and between rows)
Potatoes	30–38 cm (12–15 in) apart (in and between rows)
Peas	3 rows sown about 5 cm (2 in) apart and 5 cm (2 in) between the peas
Carrots	sow sparsely and thin to 10 cm (4 in) apart
Onions	15–30 cm (6–12 in) apart

Vegetable growing, probably more than any other form of gardening, is an art where small but vital lessons are gained through experience and experiment. Varieties which a neighbouring gardener reckons to be best for the area, may not do well for you. But this will not become apparent until you have tried and compared them and failed.

The great thing about vegetable growing, though, is that a complete flop one year could be the springboard for excellent produce the next.

Fruit

The sign of a connoisseur among the self-sufficiency group of gardeners is a thriving fruit plot. But growing a large range of fruits demands considerable space.

Top fruit
These are the fruits which grow on trees, such as apples and pears. Years ago they were only grown in large gardens or orchards, but as a result of experimental work on rootstocks smaller, quicker fruiting trees have now been produced.

The domestic apple tree is a combination of two plants – the top growth (scion) of the variety whose fruit we want, and the rootstock, which controls the vigour, and ultimate fruiting, of the plant.

Apples grafted on to very dwarfing rootstocks (M27) can even be grown in tubs, but the most popular rootstock for a small garden is the dwarfing M9.

Bush fruits
The choice of bush fruits extends beyond blackcurrants, redcurrants, gooseberries and raspberries, but all are equally simple to grow.

All fruit bushes need moisture to produce succulent fruit each season – yes, even gooseberries can be succulent and sweet! However, to ripen well, fruit needs plenty of sunshine, which is not too abundant in the North. A gardener with a south-facing wall, though, should still be able to grow superb peaches.

Pruning fruit bushes

The pruning of fruit bushes and trees causes the beginner great difficulty and aggravation. There is something about a pair of secateurs and a bush to prune that can turn a normally decisive and confident person into a quivering mass of nerves. Once his initial fear is overcome, however, he tends to become ruthless.

Autumn fruiting raspberries

These are probably the easiest of the bush fruits to prune, as they need *all* the shoots pruning almost to ground level in February.

Summer fruiting raspberries

All the canes which have produced fruit should be removed to ground level. Thin out the remainder, leaving one cane every 23–30 cm (9 in–12 in). These are fastened to wires held between poles, and can attain 2 m (6 ft) before the tip is pruned out.

Gooseberries

A good pair of leather pruning gloves is essential before you start pruning gooseberries, as they and their gardeners tend to become very attached to each other. It can be a painful liaison, particularly for the gardener!

Gooseberries can be pruned straight after fruiting, but it is more often done during the winter. As with all woody plants, fruiting or not, the first law of pruning is to remove all dead and diseased wood. Next remove the weak and spindly growths, but go steady as over-enthusiasm could result in there being nothing left of the plant. New shoots should be shortened by at least a third, and all crossing branches removed, leaving the plant with a round headed top and an open centre.

Redcurrants and whitecurrants

Pruning is virtually the same as for gooseberries, except that gloves are not essential.

Strawberries

Little can match the taste of the season's first strawberries. Just ask any blackbird as he raids the new crop! Protection is essential to prevent bird attack. Netting is the best method, but it is not sufficient just to rest the netting on top of the fruit crop. It must be held aloft on wires or poles.

Strawberries tend to hug the soil, which makes the fruits dirty and also tends to encourage disease. To keep them clean, spread a layer of straw for them to rest on.

All fruits are expensive early (and late) in the season. An excellent way of producing strawberries early when they are especially appreciated is to grow them in pots.

Plant them around the edge of an 18 cm (7 in), 20 cm (8 in), or 25 cm (10 in) plant pot in John Innes No. 2 compost, and leave them outside in the cold until February. By this time the cold weather will have initiated flower buds. If they can then be brought into a cold greenhouse and stacked on top of each other, this will save space, and enable you to grow far more strawberries.

Even in a cold greenhouse they will flower long before their outdoor relations, but as the bees are not yet active their flowers will need pollinating. Use a *clean* paintbrush to give each flower a little tickle in turn, taking pollen from one flower to the next. Successfully pollinated, the strawberries should then 'set', and the resulting fruits cascade down the sides of the plant pots, staying perfectly clean *and* ready a fortnight before your neighbours'!

Herbs

Herbs have enjoyed a revival in recent years, and are now a growth industry. While it is their value in the kitchen that has brought about this new-found popularity, they are also a pleasure to grow. The fragrance of the flowers and foliage as well as their beauty makes them an attractive and useful addition to beds and borders. The many varieties of thyme and marjoram are good groundcover plants, besides being ideal on a rock garden or in paving.

Most of the herbs we grow are from warm climates, so when choosing a site for them, find a sheltered, sunny spot. Reflected heat from buildings can be an added bonus, which is why many garden herbs are grown in gaps in paving.

If creating a herb garden, site it near the kitchen. Most busy cooks will not appreciate a 100-yard dash to pick the herb of the day! Alternatively herbs can be grown in tubs or barrels. They appreciate a well drained compost where they can put their feet in the sand and lie back in the sunshine.

So if tarragon makes your taste buds tingle, and parsley is poetry to your palate, be sure to include herbs somewhere in your garden.

SEASONAL GUIDE

12

One of the most frequent questions gardeners are asked is, 'When is the *best time* to sow . . . prune . . . plant, etc?' about virtually every job in the garden. The stock replies tend to be 'The best time is generally three o'clock on a Saturday afternoon!', or 'Whenever you have the time to do the job.' Both evade the detail the questioner requires, but they do make the point that there is a degree of flexibility about the best time.

Gardeners have to be able to work with fluctuating seasonal weather. When it throws its worst at us we can at least retreat indoors for protection. But plants are rooted to the spot and unable to join us by the fireside (except for a few pot plants), and have to stay outside suffering from wind and frosted tips!

In sheltered regions a winter in the garden may not be too hard to bear, but in the North plants do need protection from frost. Shelter and sensible growing techniques are vital, but timing can be crucial. By delaying pruning or planting an extra couple of weeks compared with the South saves plants considerable unwanted hardship.

However, it is far better to use the 'Manual of Commonsense' in conjunction with any seasonal guide, because the seasons vary slightly from one year to the next.

WINTER

	GREENHOUSE	GARDEN	LAWN
JAN	Keep pot plants on the dry side and free from dead leaves	Check tree ties and rabbit guards	Keep off lawns when frozen
	Good greenhouse hygiene essential throughout the winter	Have all machinery serviced in time for the next season	Remove debris
		Remove any old trees and shrubs past their best and plant replacements when conditions allow	
		Lightly fork borders, being careful not to damage roots	
FEB	Sow half-hardy annuals under glass	Apply weedkillers such as Simazine to paths and beds where suitable	
		Start sowing vegetable seeds under cloches or in frame which gives protection	
		Mulch garden as necessary	
MARCH	Start taking cuttings of new shoots	Prune bush and fan-trained fruit such as peaches	Lightly rake and brush the lawn
		Prune roses if not already done in autumn	

SPRING

	GREENHOUSE	GARDEN	LAWN
APRIL	Pot up rootbound plants

Sow seeds for continued summer display

Begin liquid feeding | Stake herbaceous plants with twigs when growth is 15 cm (6in) high | Give lawn a light rolling after clearing winter debris

First cut should merely 'top' the lawn |
| **MAY** | Take tops out of pot plants to keep them bushy. Some can be used as cuttings to propagate more | 'Harden off' bedding plants in a cold frame, covering at night if frosty

Plant out dahlias

Leave bulb foliage for 6 weeks after flowering before removing

Plant aquatics during their growing season | Feed and weedkill lawns |
| **JUNE** | | Plant summer bedding plants after frosts have ceased

Start summer propagating, taking cuttings of shrubs as new growth becomes suitable | |

SUMMER

	GREENHOUSE	GARDEN	LAWN
JULY	Summer prune fruit under glass, removing unwanted growing tips

Keep feeding and watering – essential throughout summer

Dead-head flowers to keep plants growing rather than seeding | In vegetable garden grow lettuces and radishes between rows of slower maturing plants

Check herbaceous plants periodically. Stake and tie with string if necessary

Tie in climbing plants before growths get too long

Find some time to sunbathe! | Frequent mowing

Water during drought; raise height of cut |

SUMMER Cont

	GREENHOUSE	GARDEN	LAWN
AUG	Check for pests and diseases and spray as necessary Propagate as necessary throughout the summer It becomes more difficult to root cuttings as autumn approaches	Summer prune fruit – 'stopping' vegetative shoots to encourage fruit development Water pots, tubs and troughs thoroughly. Water shrubs in their first season too Trim hedges – narrow at the top. Wedge shape helps them shed snow which could otherwise damage the hedge	Continue to weed and feed until September
SEPT		Aphids on aquatics should be washed off with hose-pipe. They make good fish food! Check all plants for pests and diseases and spray as necessary Plunge hyacinths for Christmas. They take 16 weeks to flower Plant outdoor bulbs	Ideal time to sow a new lawn

AUTUMN

	GREENHOUSE	GARDEN	LAWN
OCT	Reduce watering of pot plants. No more potting up Clean greenhouse glass	Protect berries with netting Protect slightly tender plants with an igloo of straw or yew branches	Raise height of cut for last few mowings Turf any bare spots on new lawn
NOV	Clean off dead or diseased leaves of pot plants to discourage infection	Lift dahlias after first frost blackens the leaves. Herbaceous plants can be cut down, lifted and divided – or left until spring Dig vegetable plot where possible, spreading farmyard manure if rotation permits	Begin autumn renovations, scarifying, spiking
DEC	Prune fruit under glass Take a chair and seed catalogues into the tropical greenhouse and plan next year's display!	Plant trees and shrubs before worst of winter sets in Start winter pruning of bush fruit. Prune roses if preferred to spring pruning *Have a happy Christmas!*	

INDEX